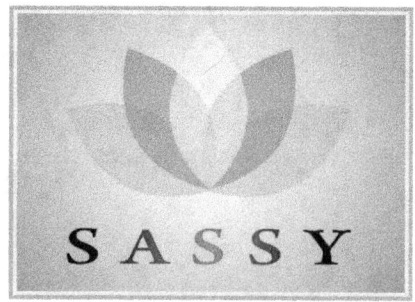

HAND DRAWN BY

SASKJA COOK

What better way to relax than to colour.
Whether you're looking for a way to unwind or a new hobby, colour therapy has been proven to be an effective stress management technique.

I love to draw and I love to see my pieces brought to life by each colourists unique take on them. Each piece is a collaboration between us, my drawing and your colouring.

Please feel free to share any finished pieces on:

www.facebook.com/sassycolouring

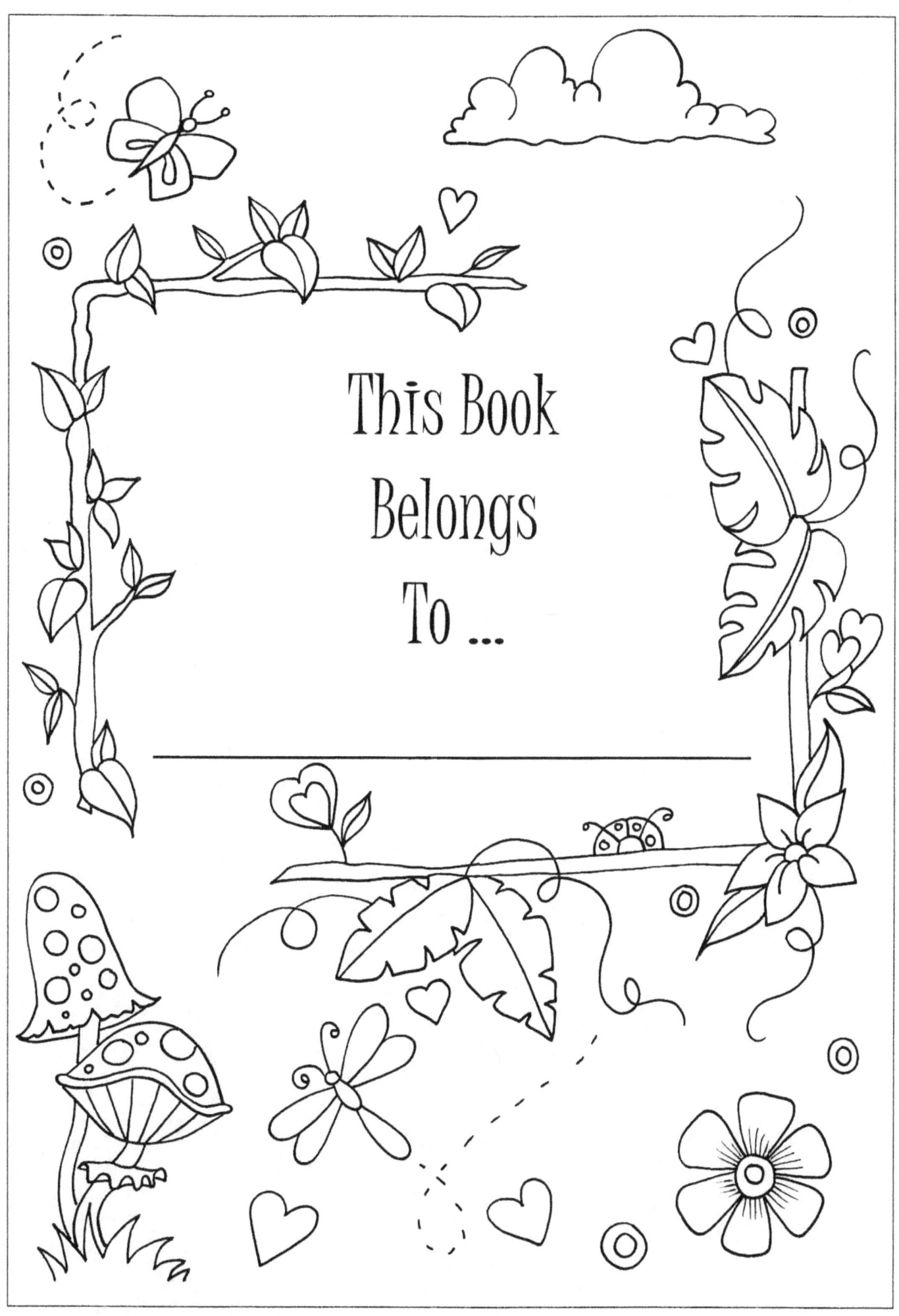

This Book

Belongs

To ...

_____

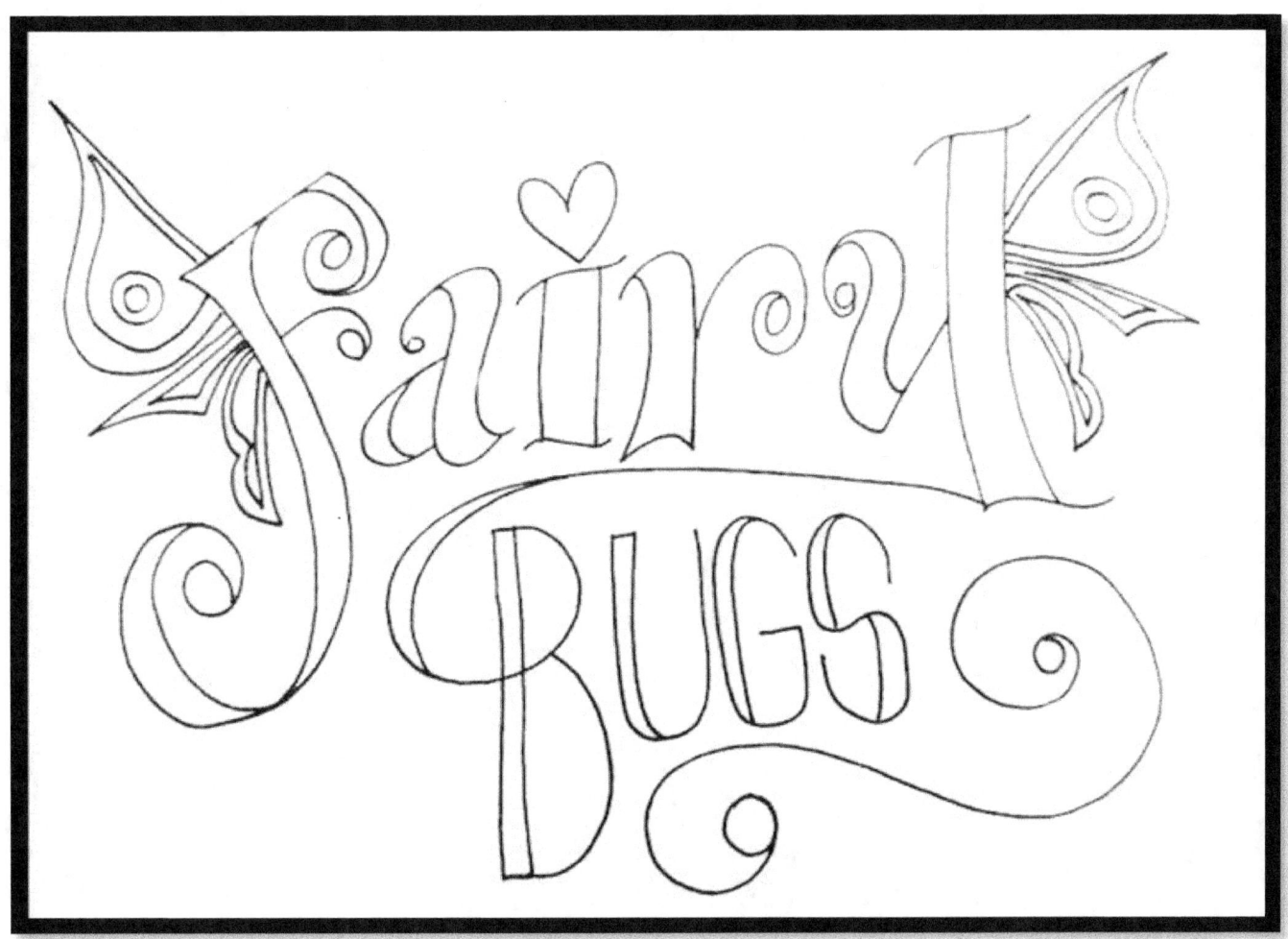

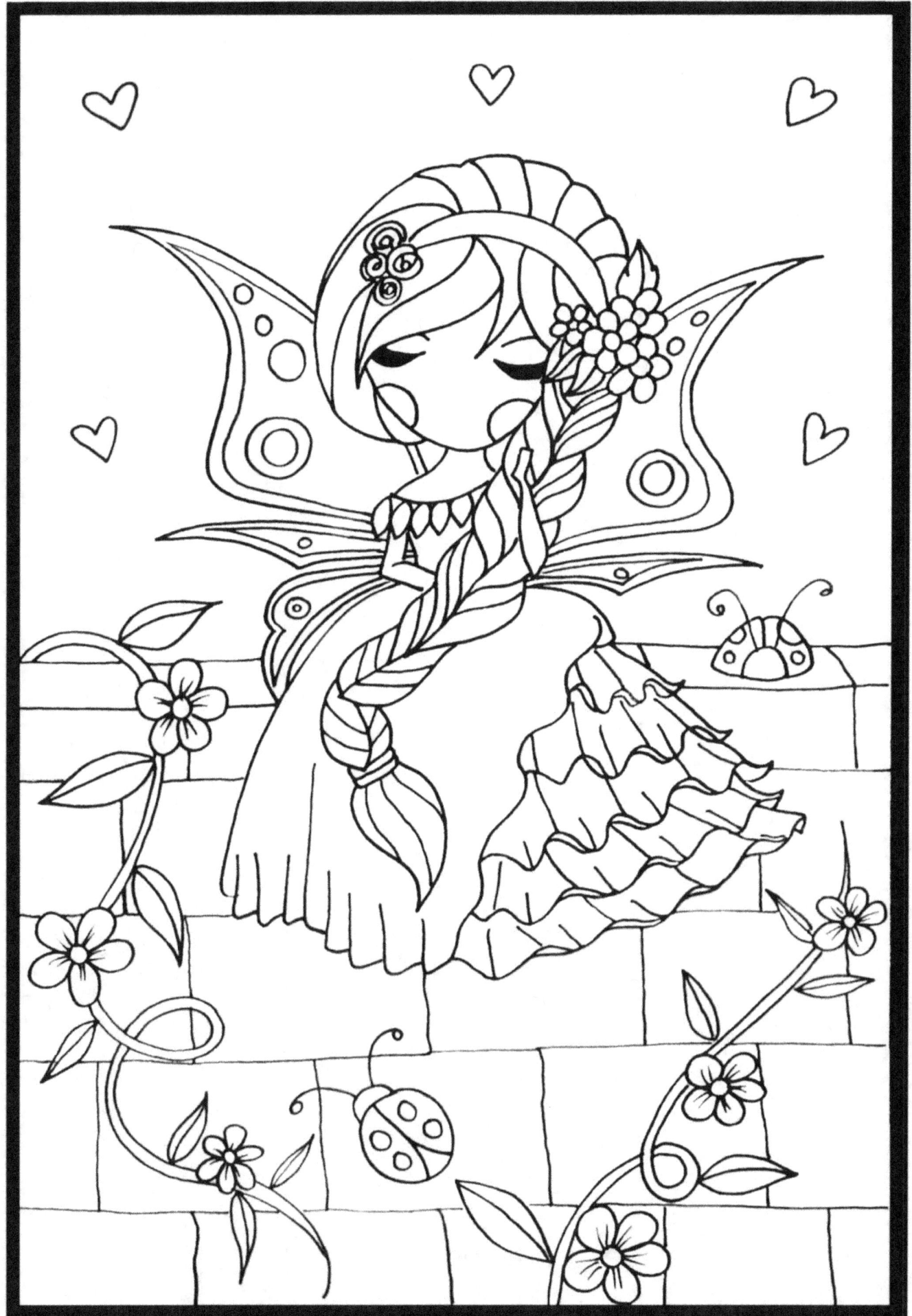

Leila and her Ladybugs

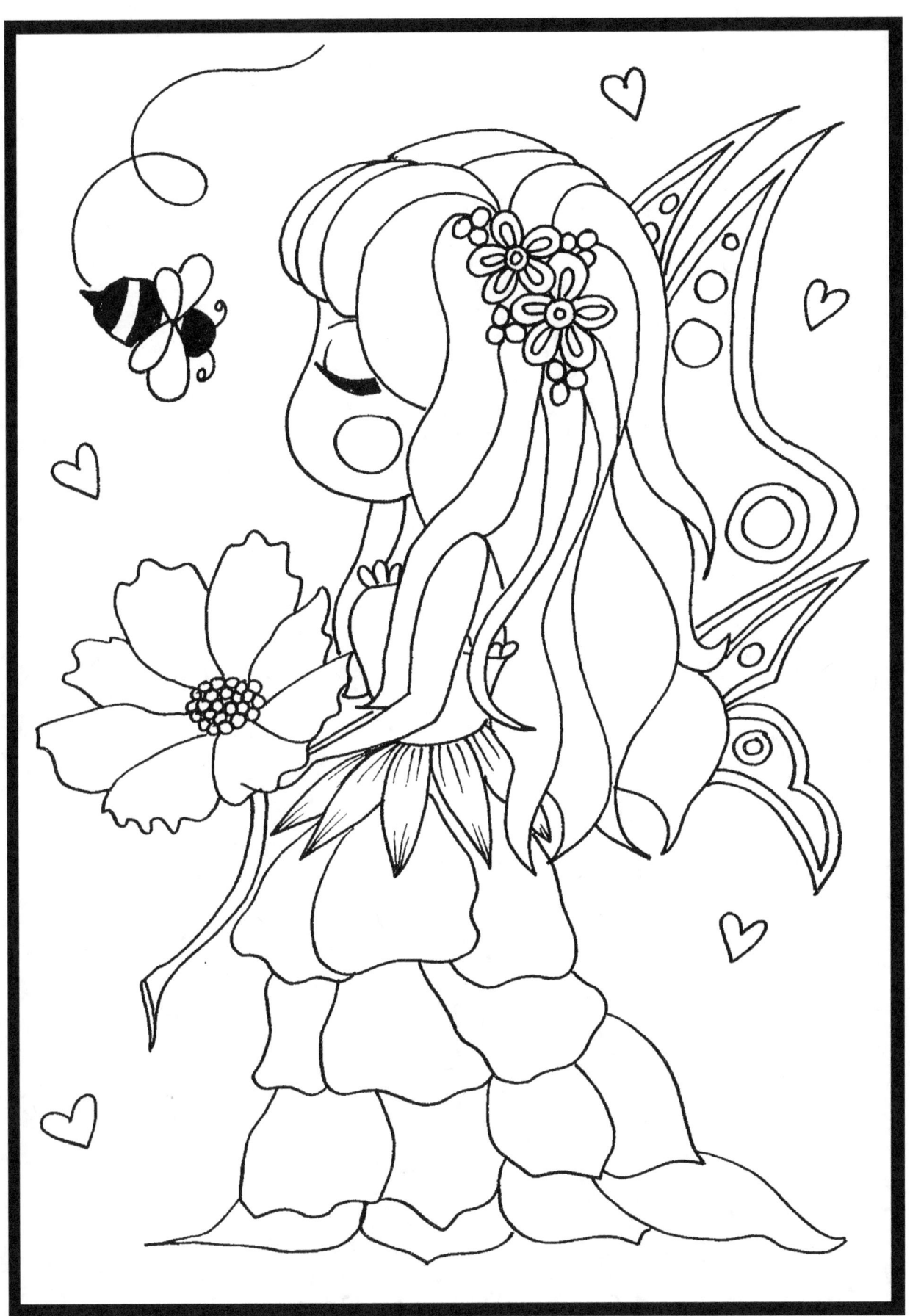

Betsy and her Bee

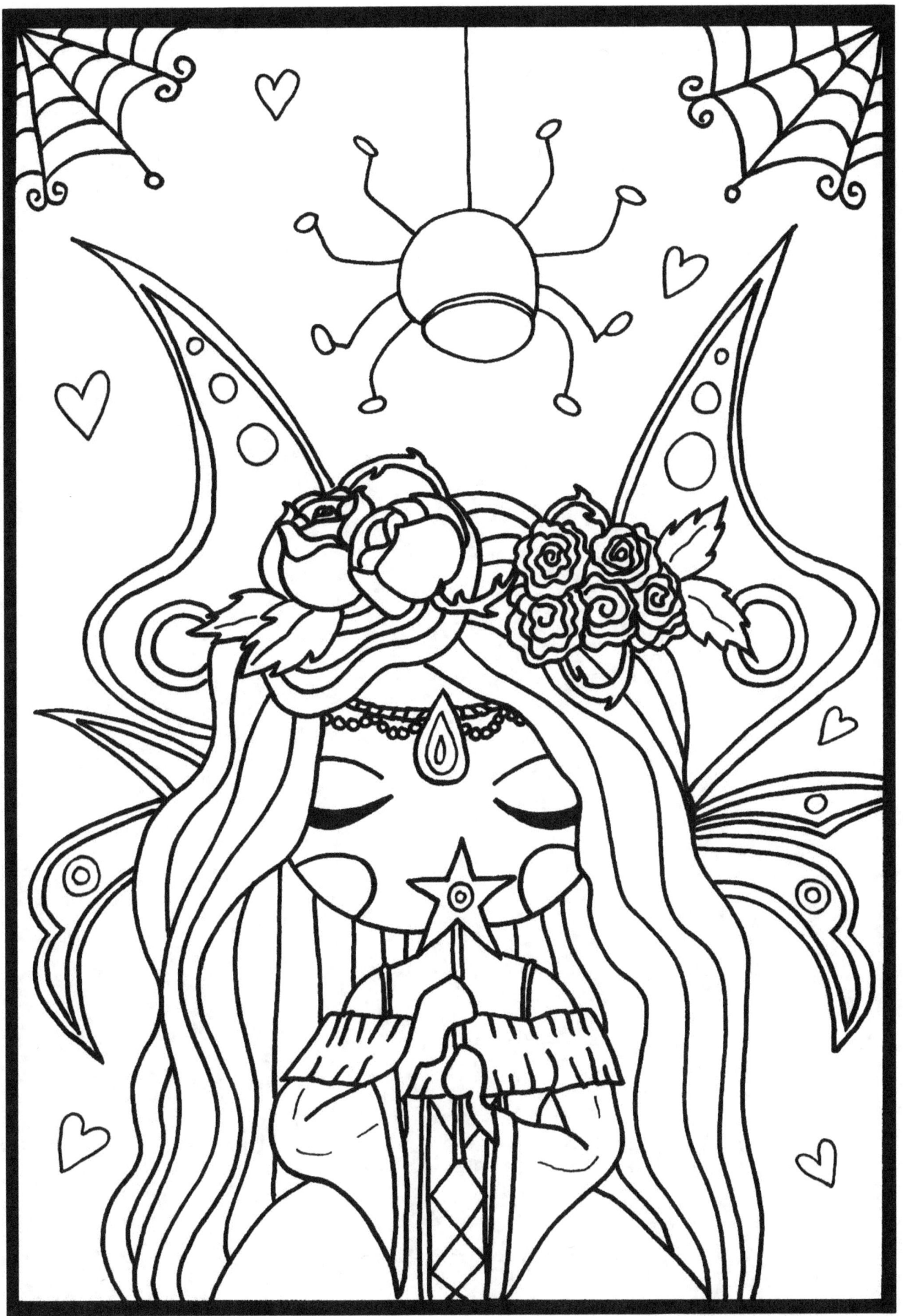

Sienna and her Spider

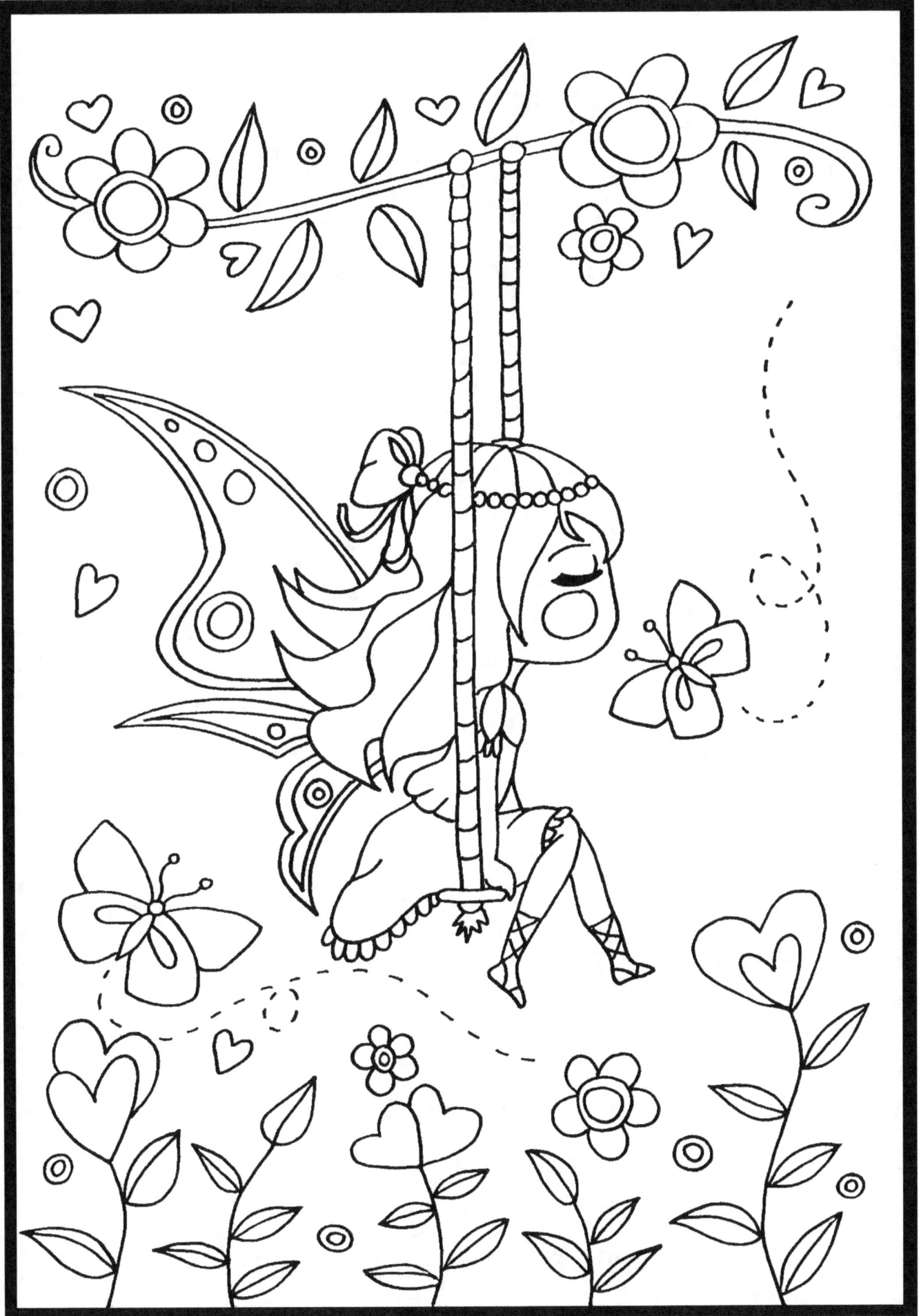

Bella and her Butterflies

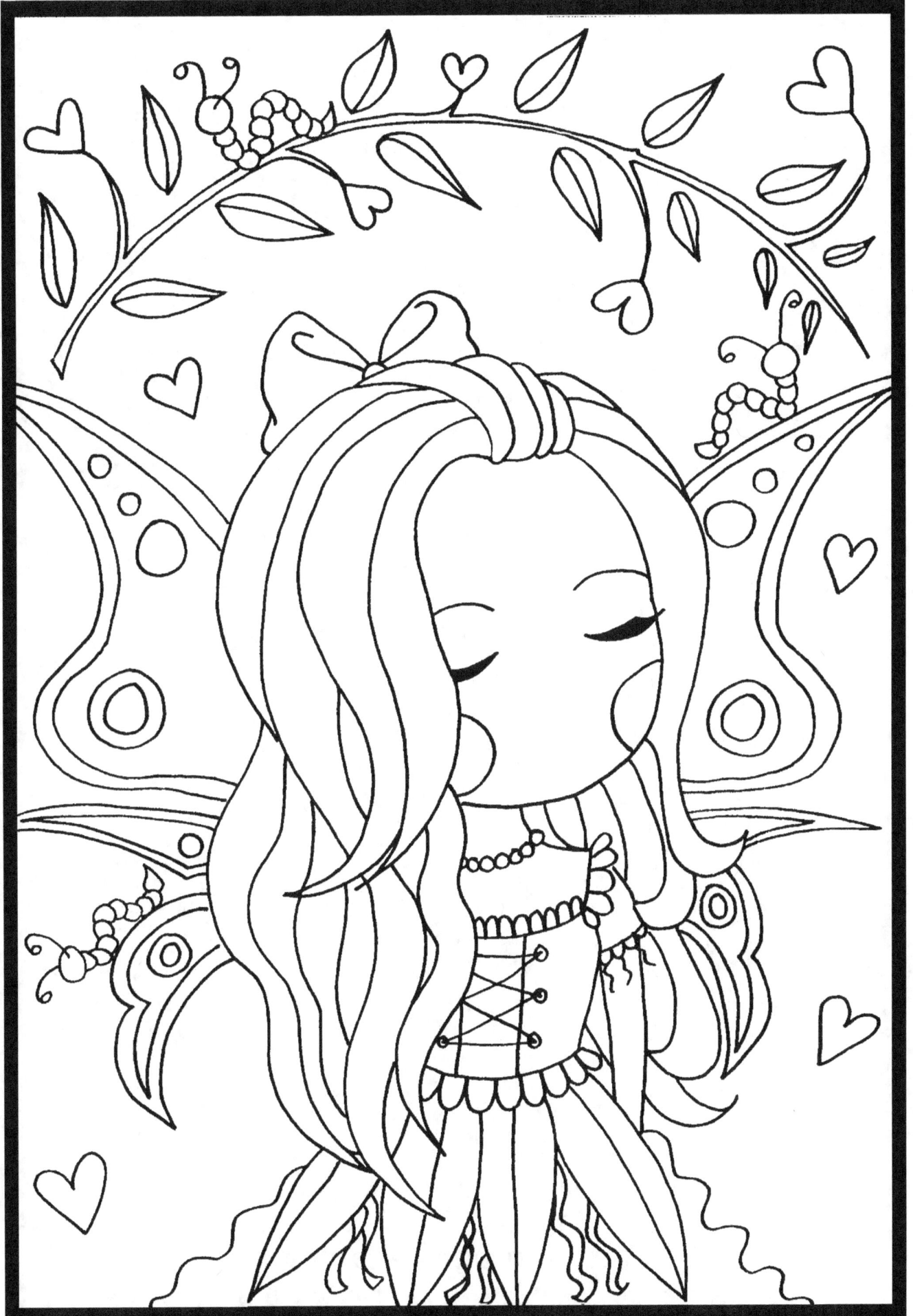

Cara and her Catapillars

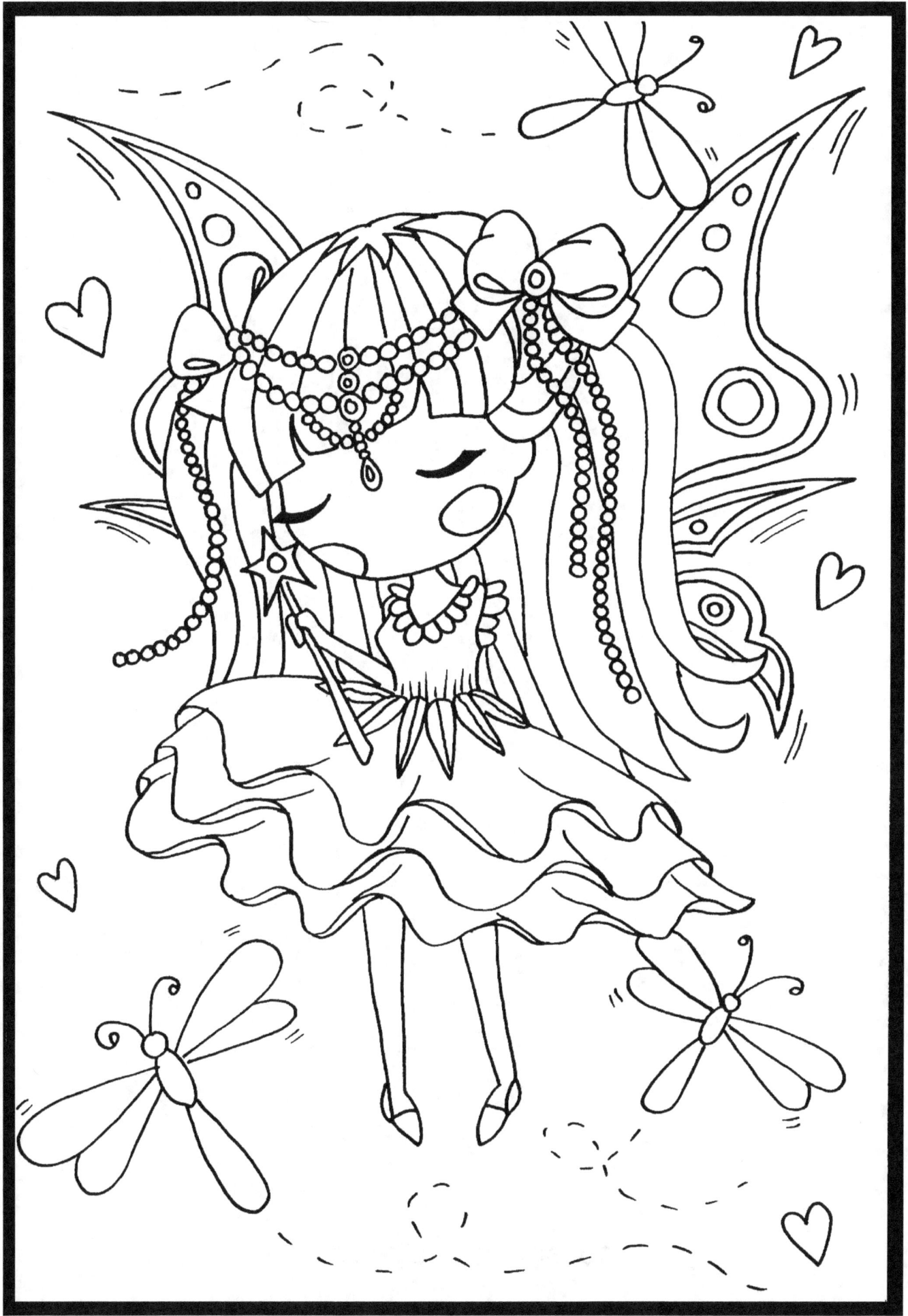

Drina and her Dragonflies

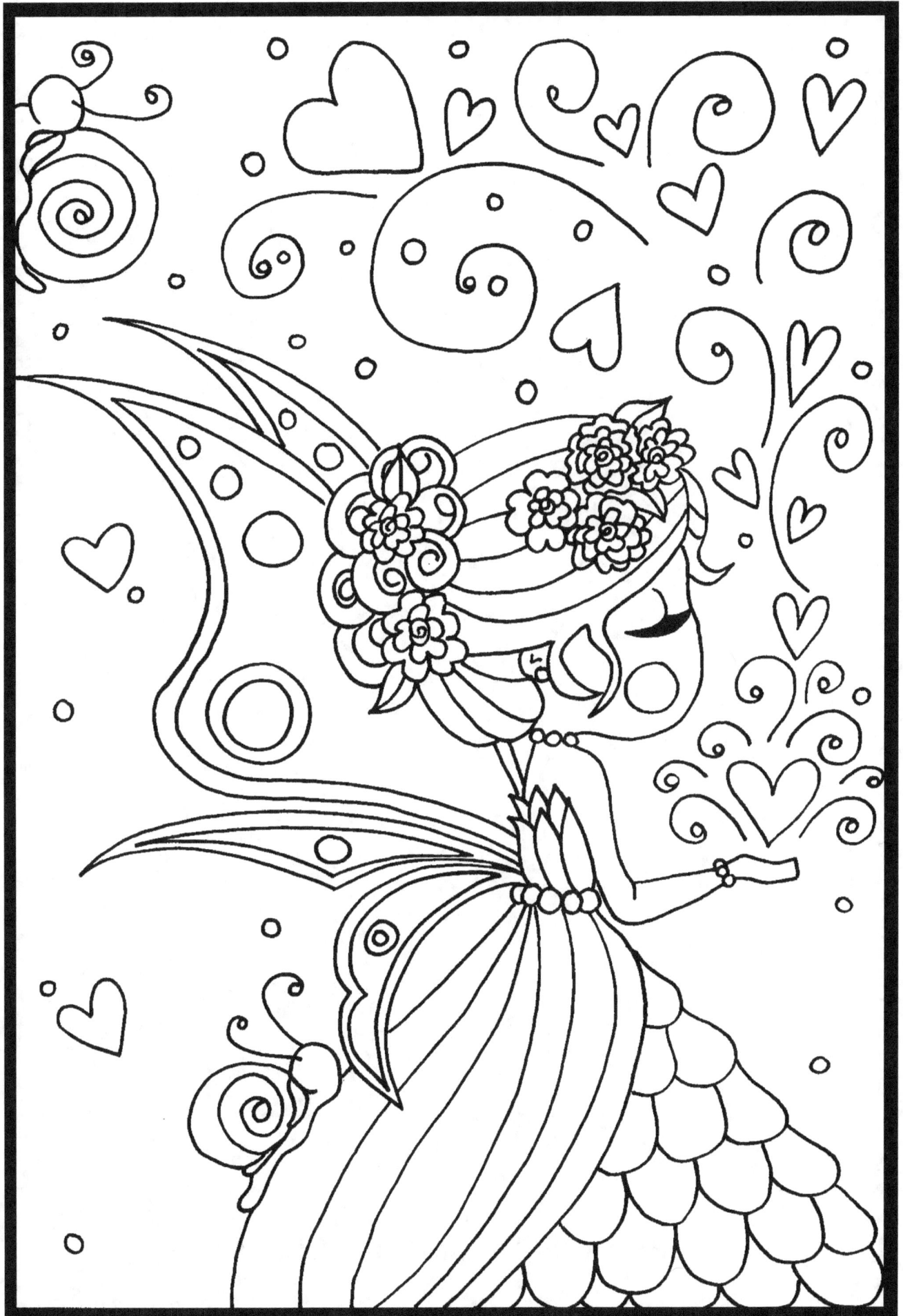

Serendipity and her Snails

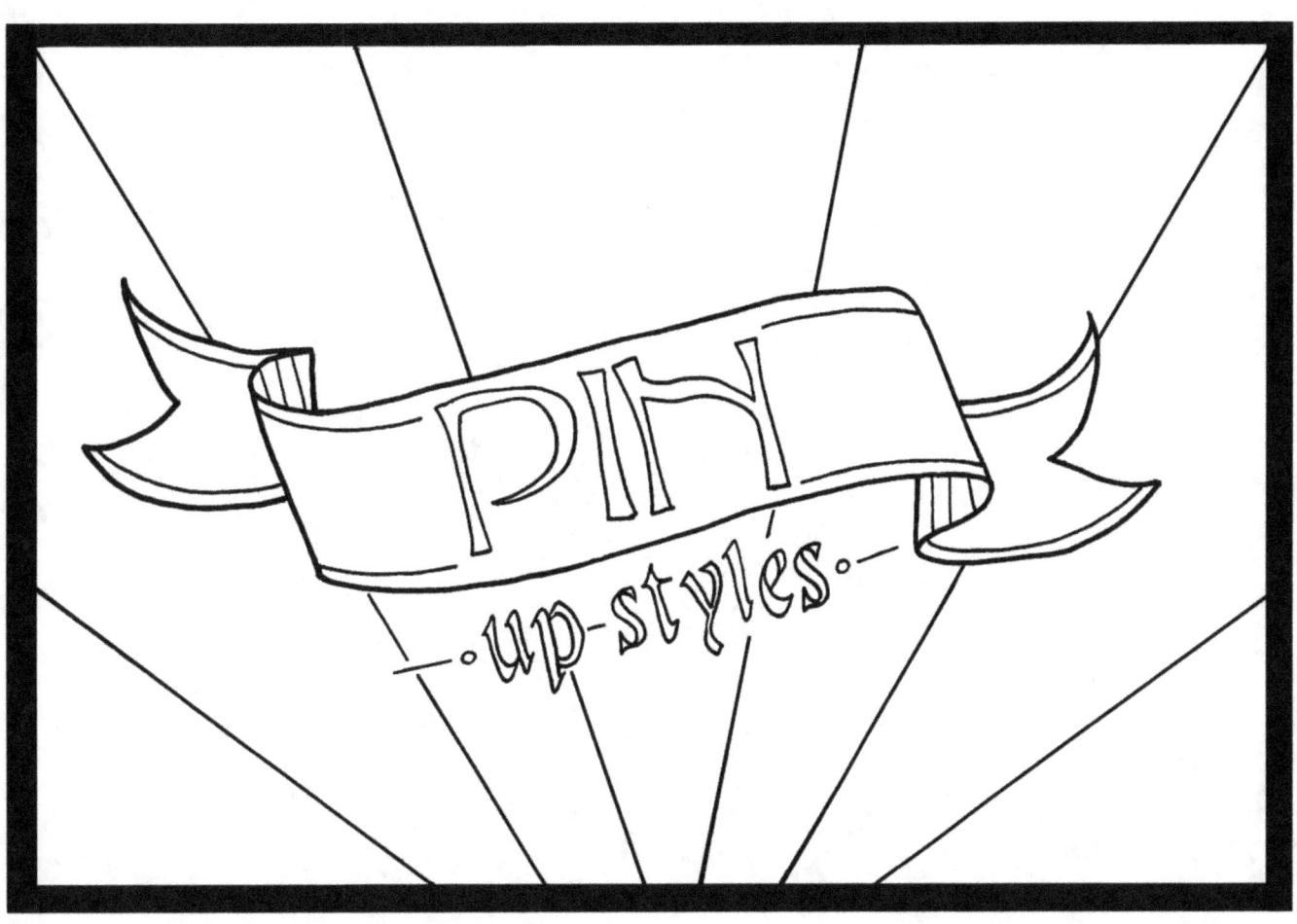

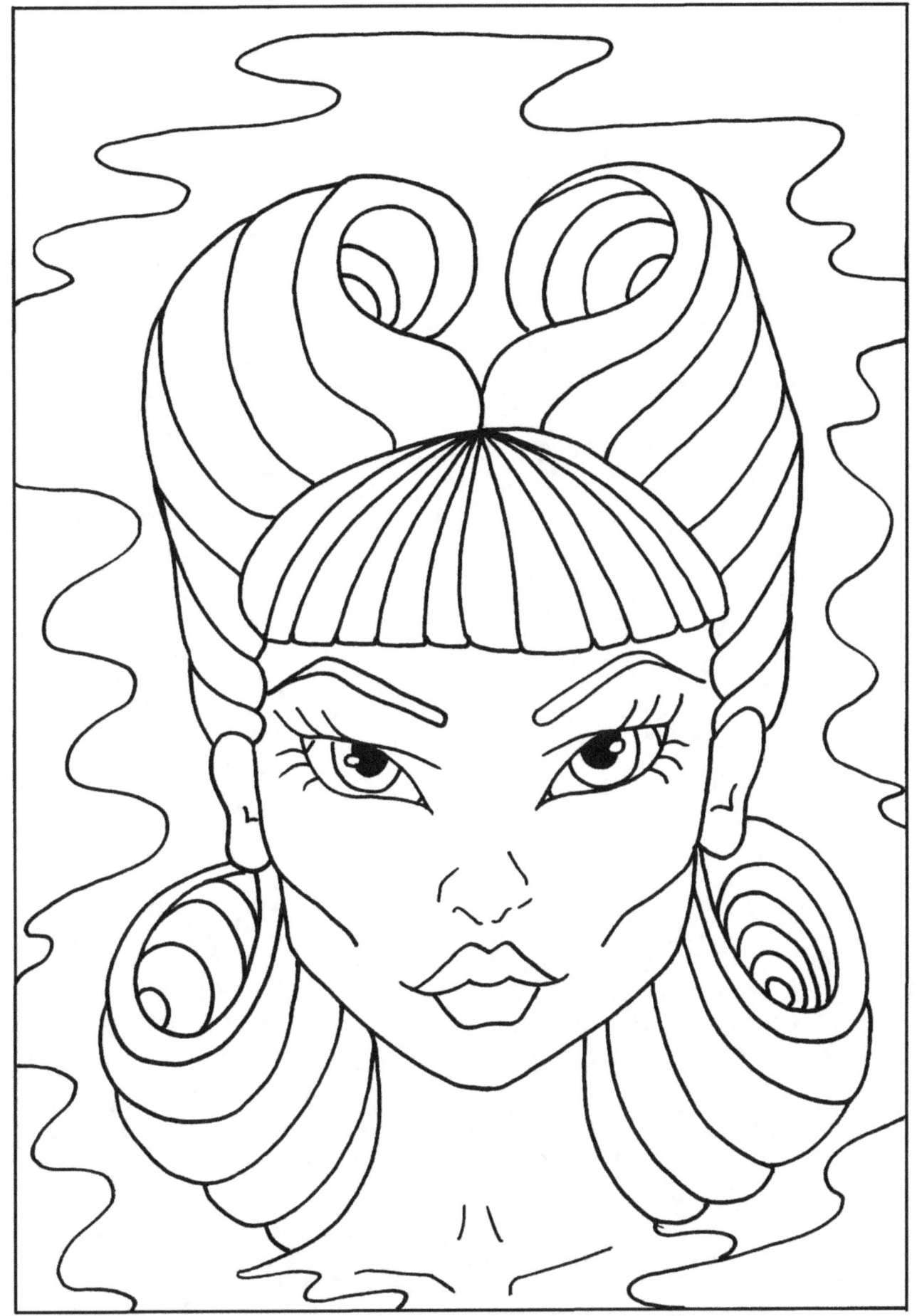

Ash

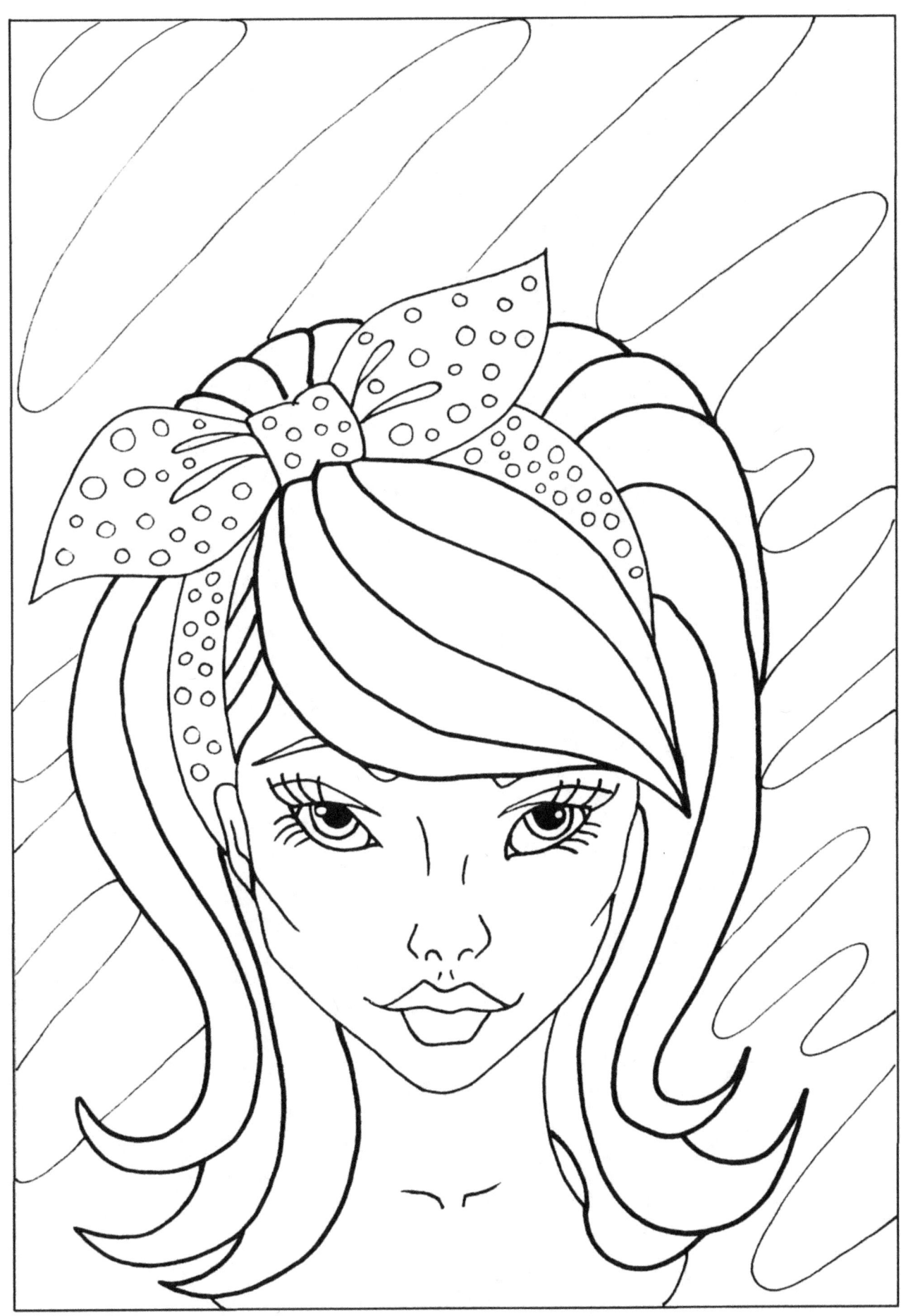

Cindy

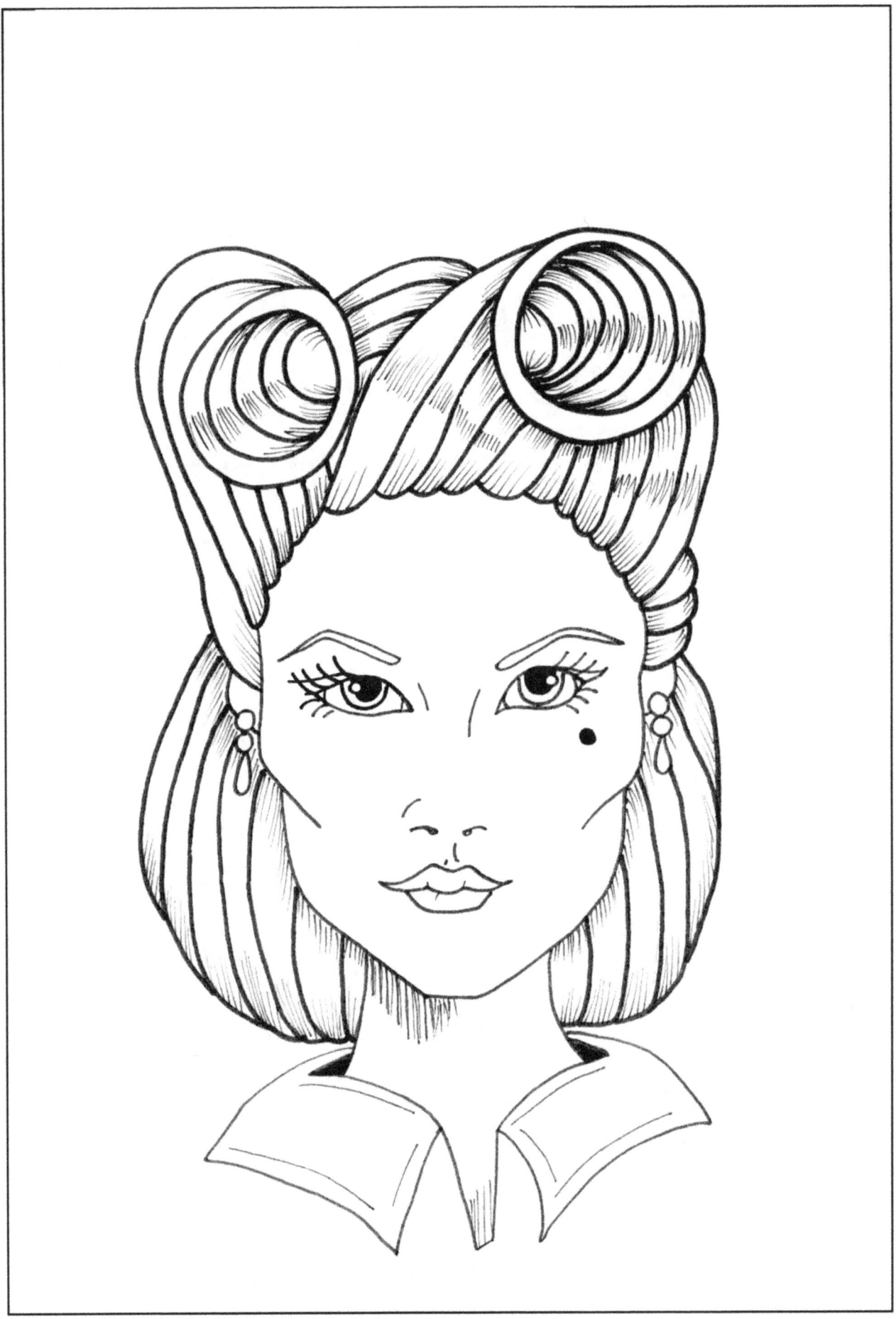

Darla

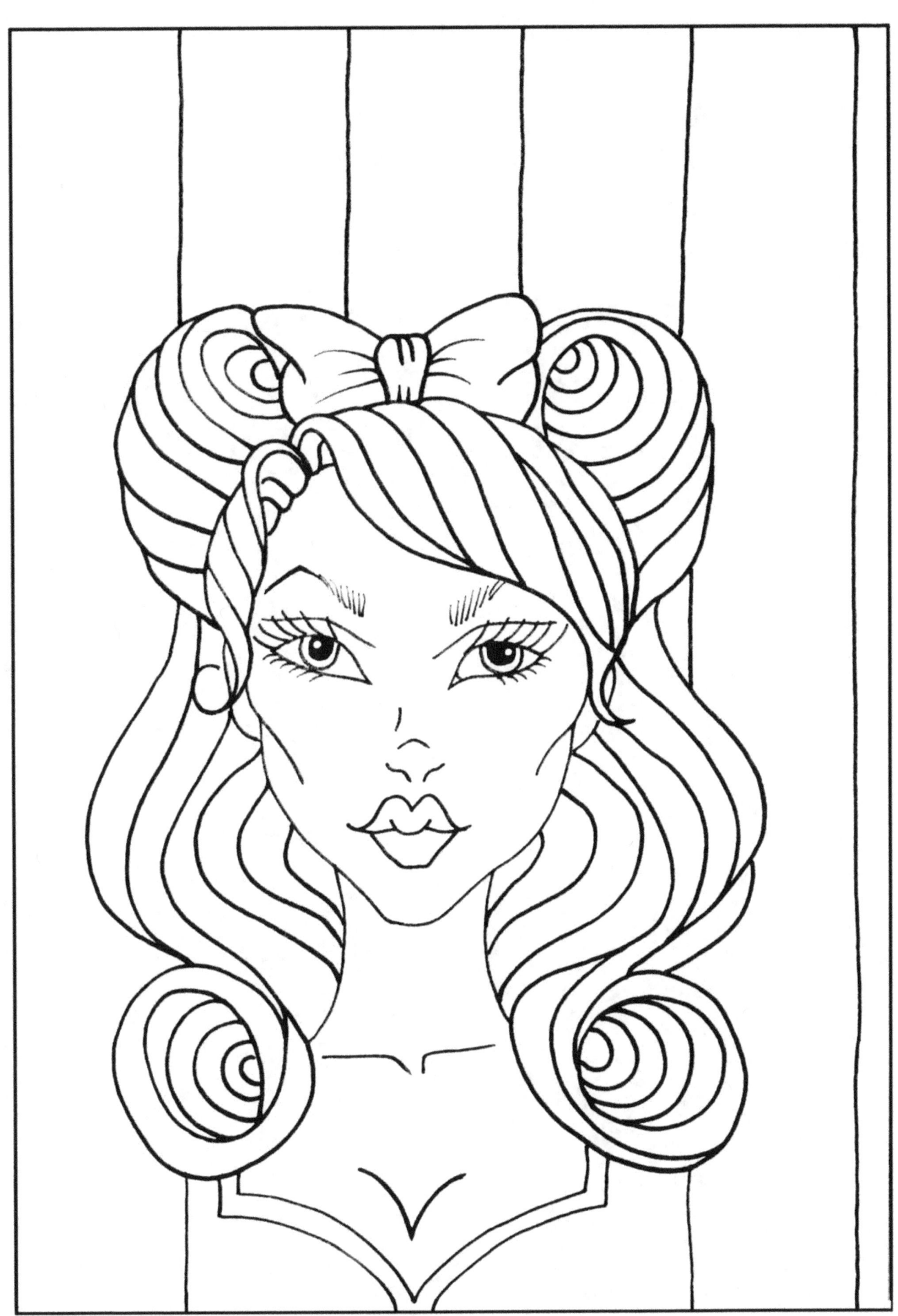

Emz

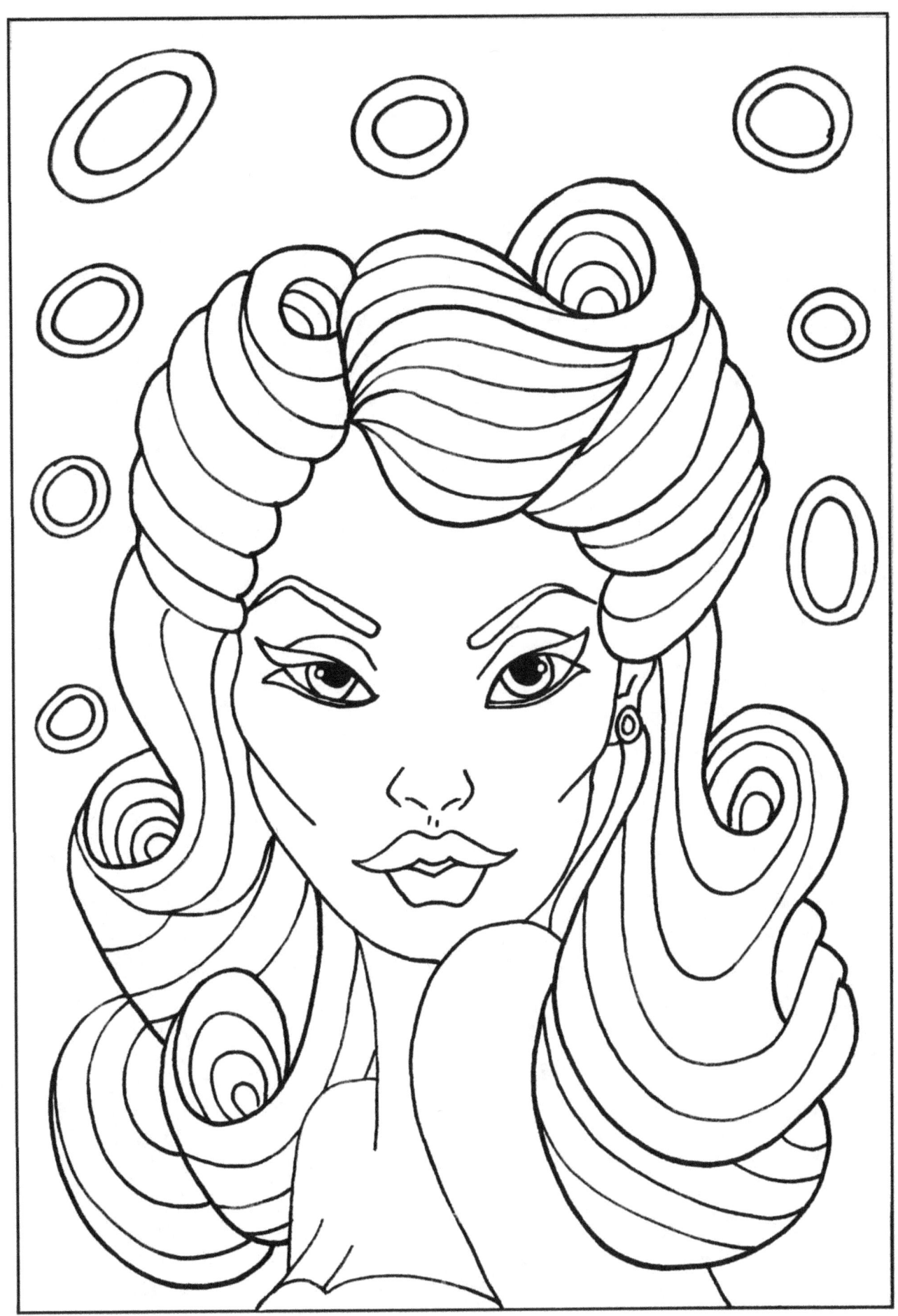

Jess

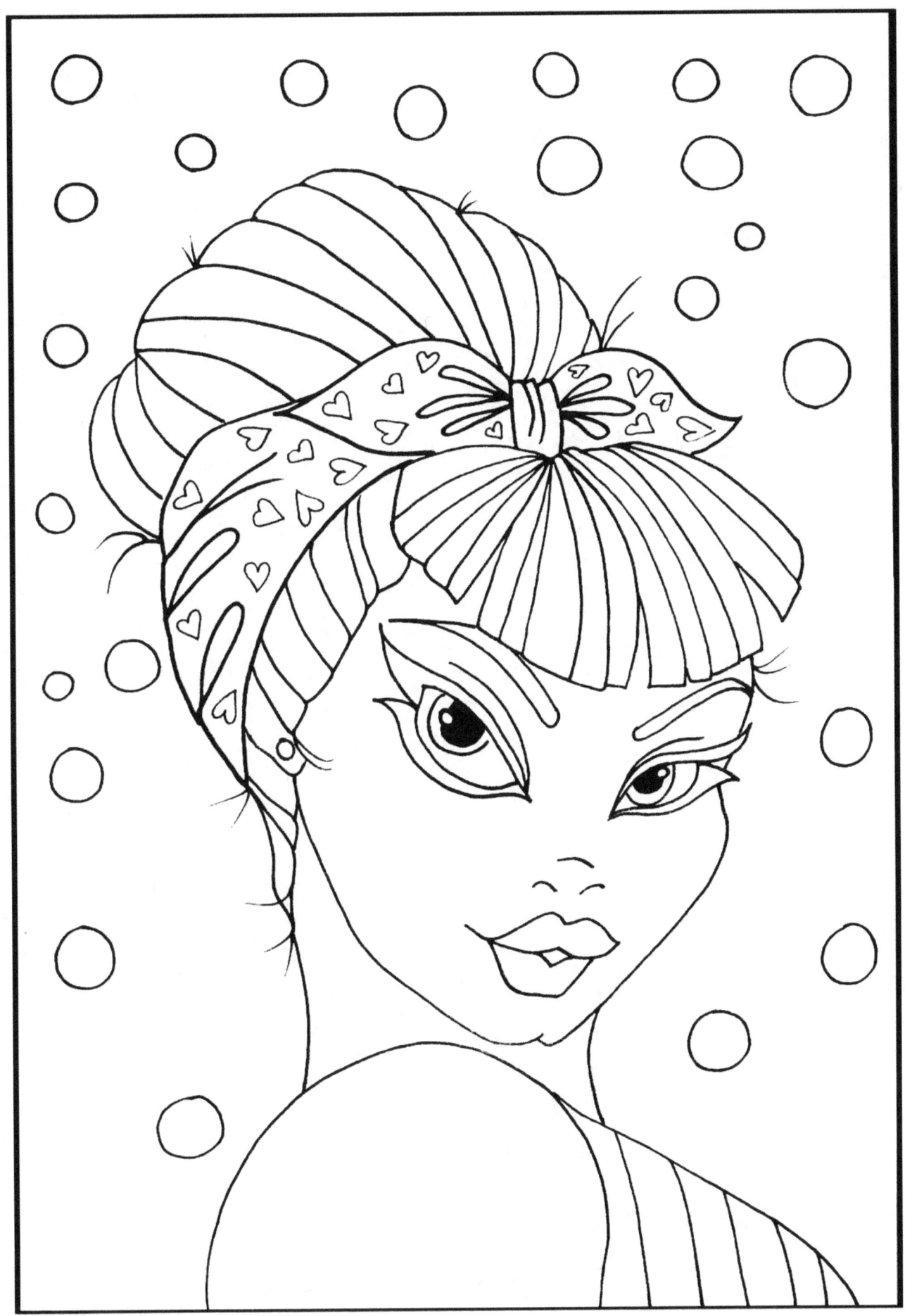

Shell

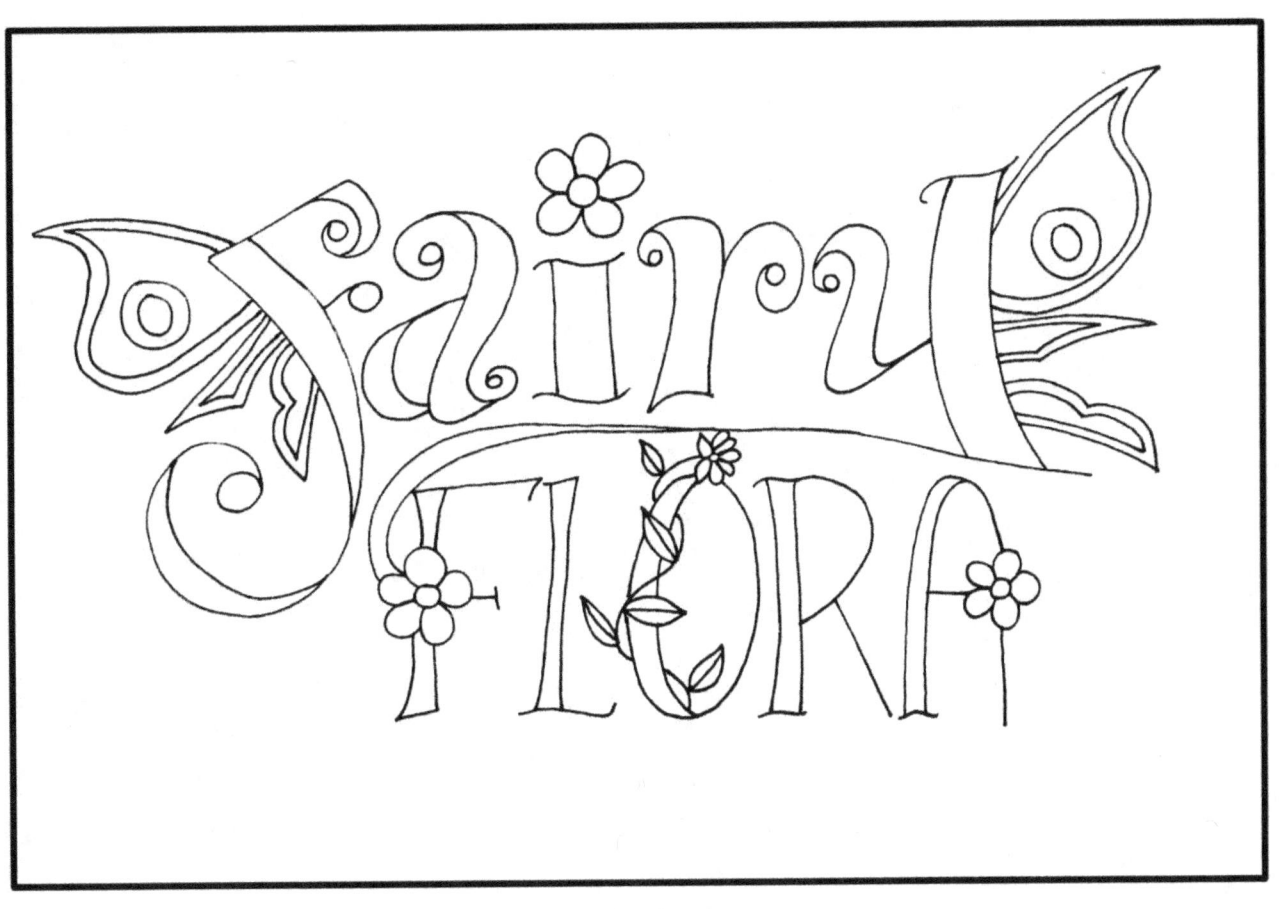

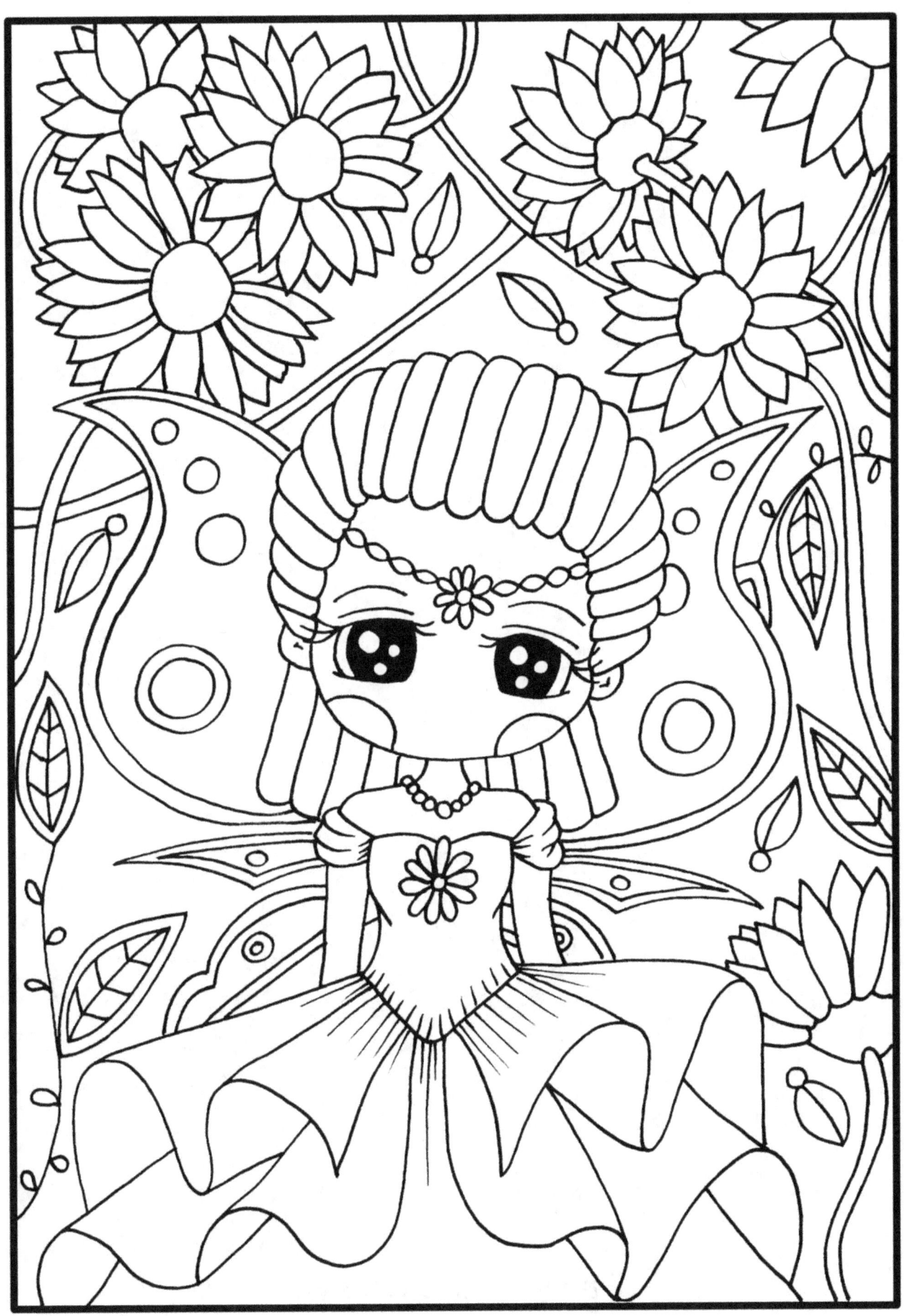

Daisy in the Daisys

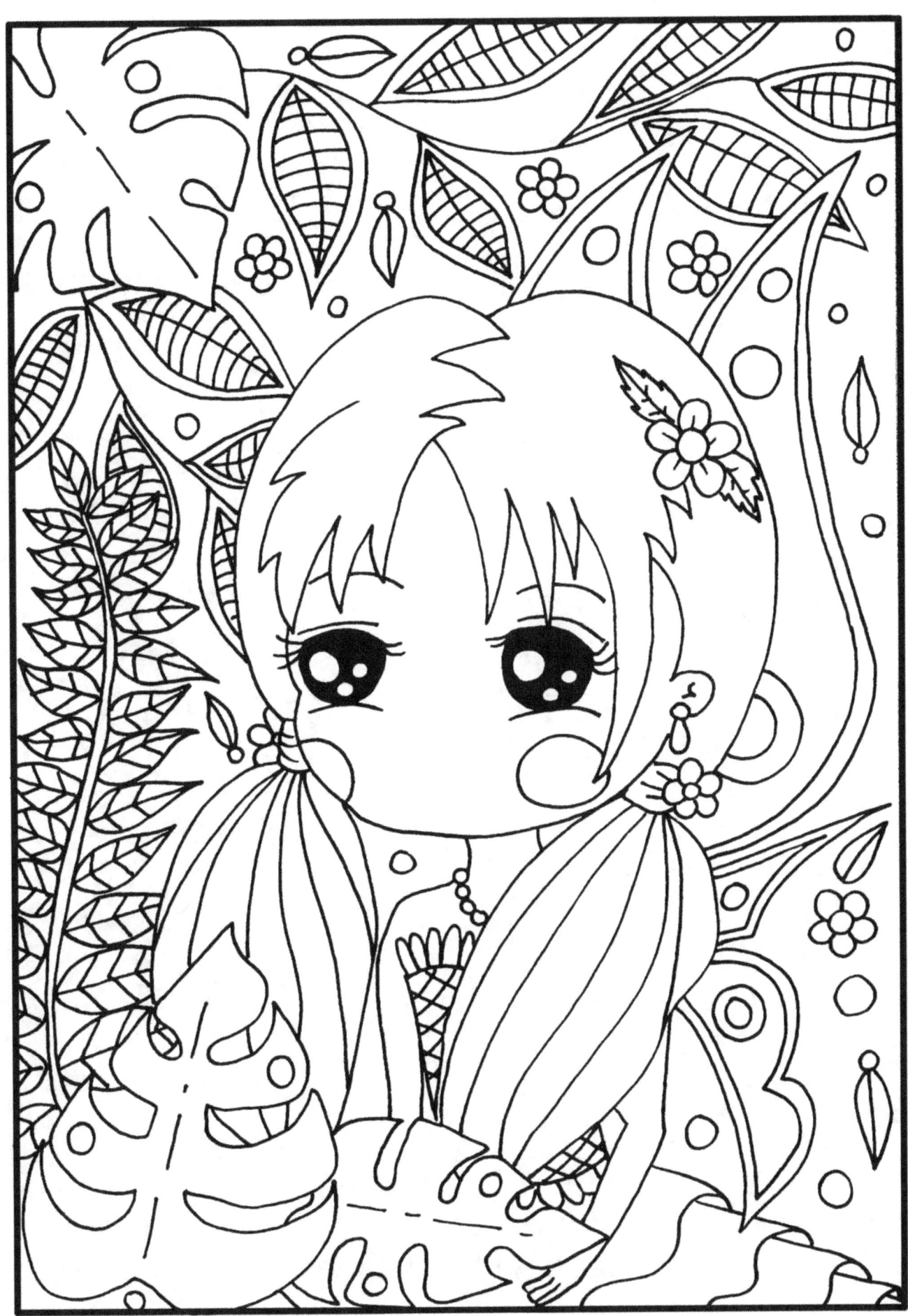

Lexie in the Leaves

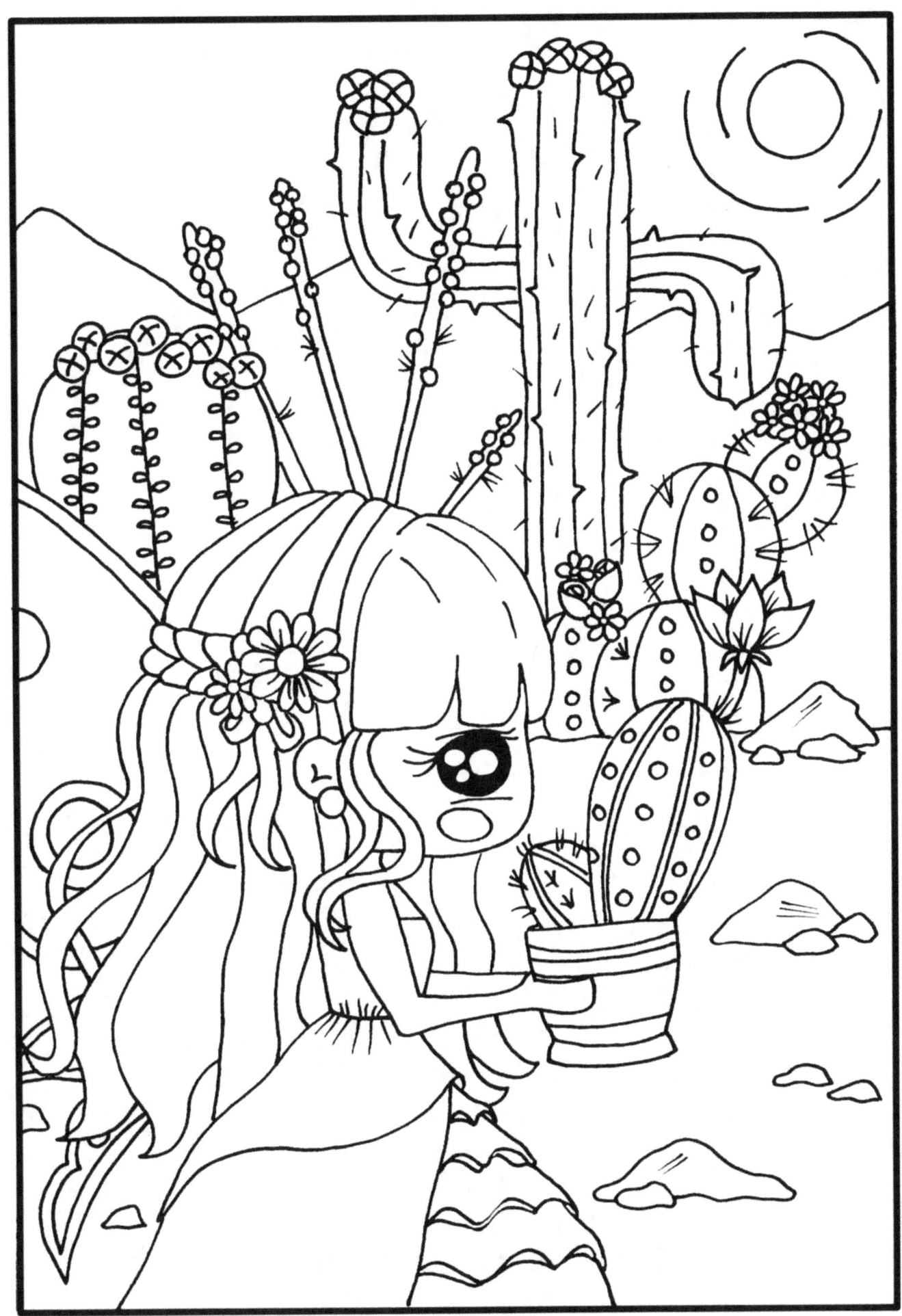

Caoimhe with the Cactus

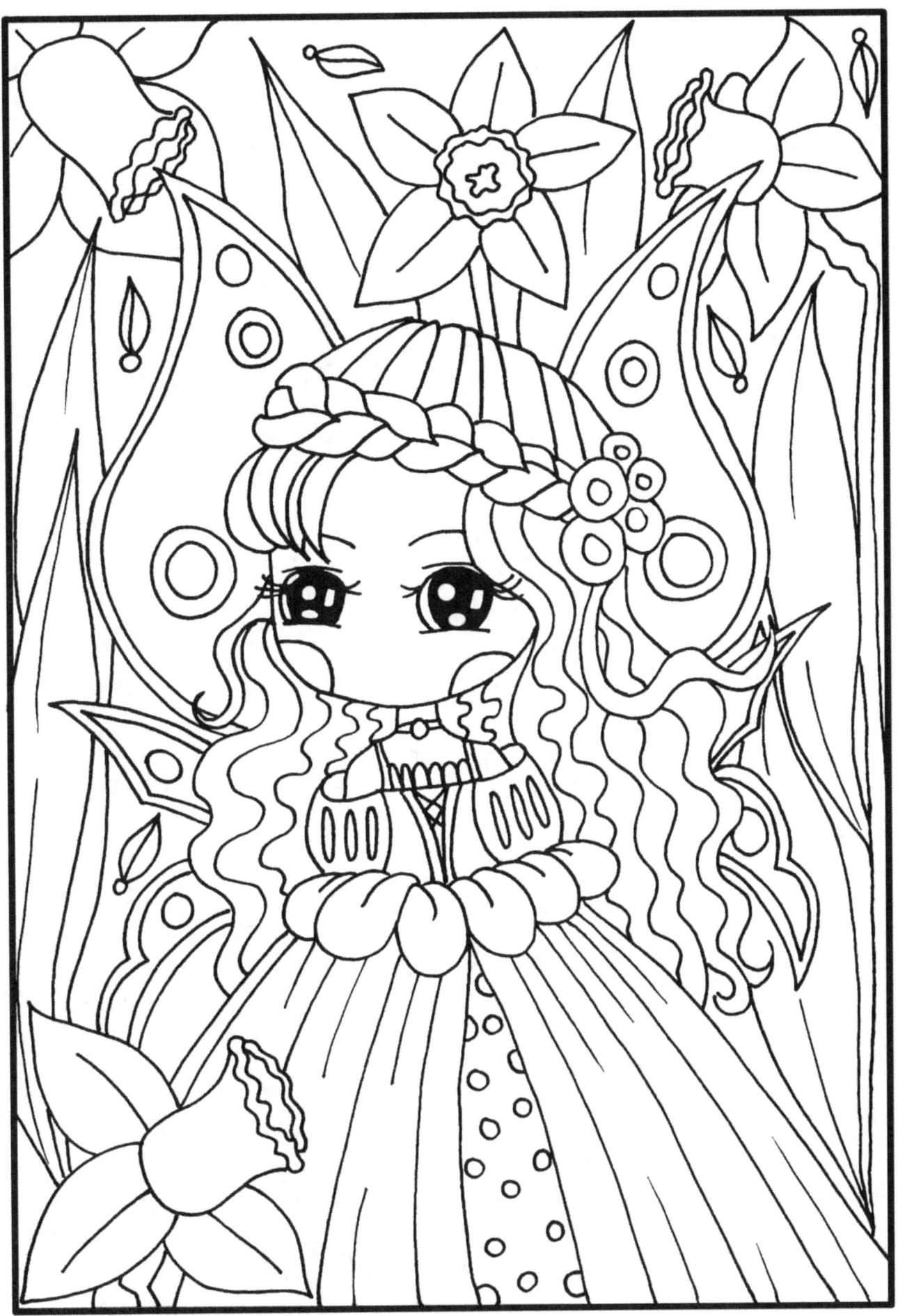

Daphne in the Daffodils

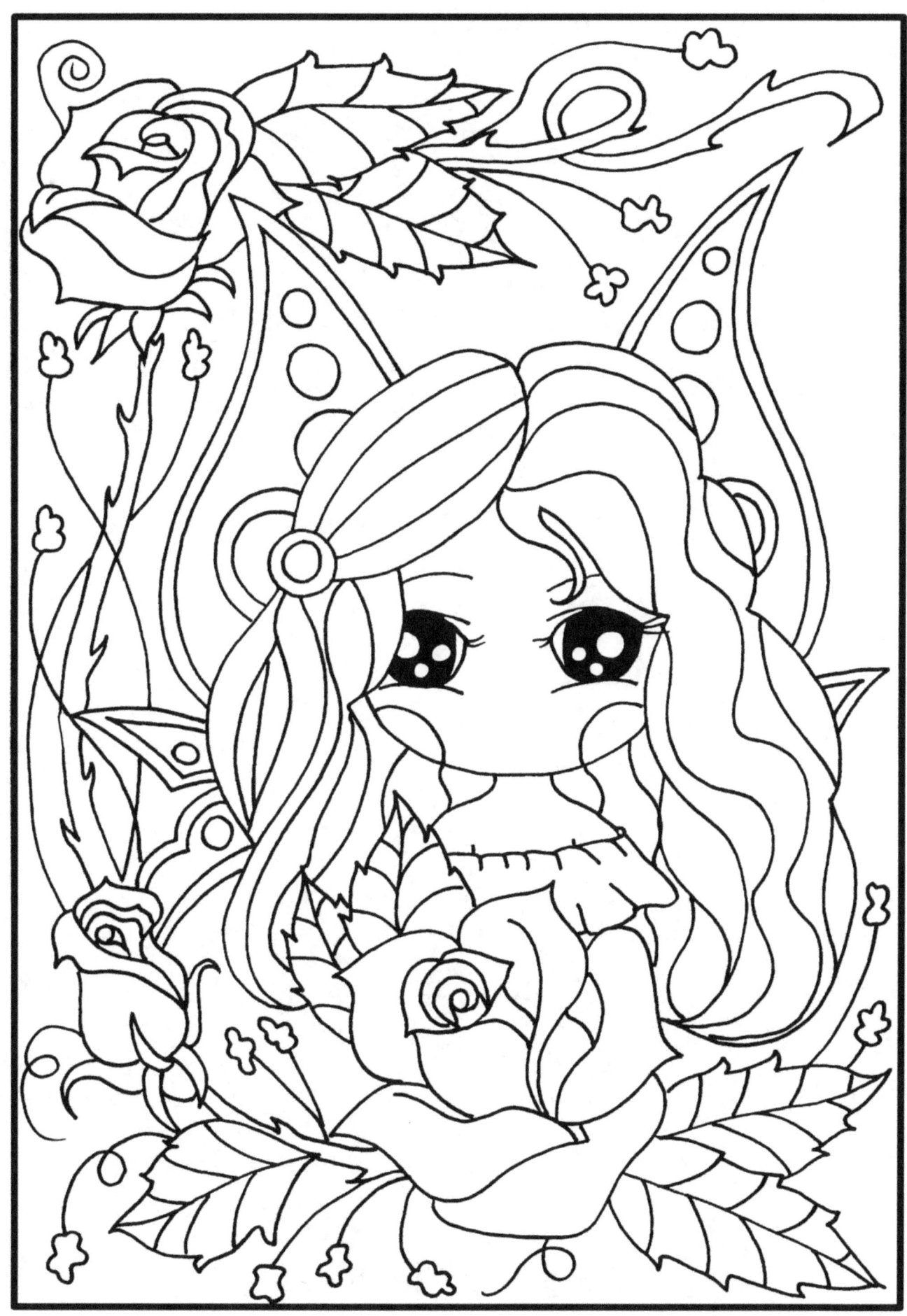

Reagan in the Roses

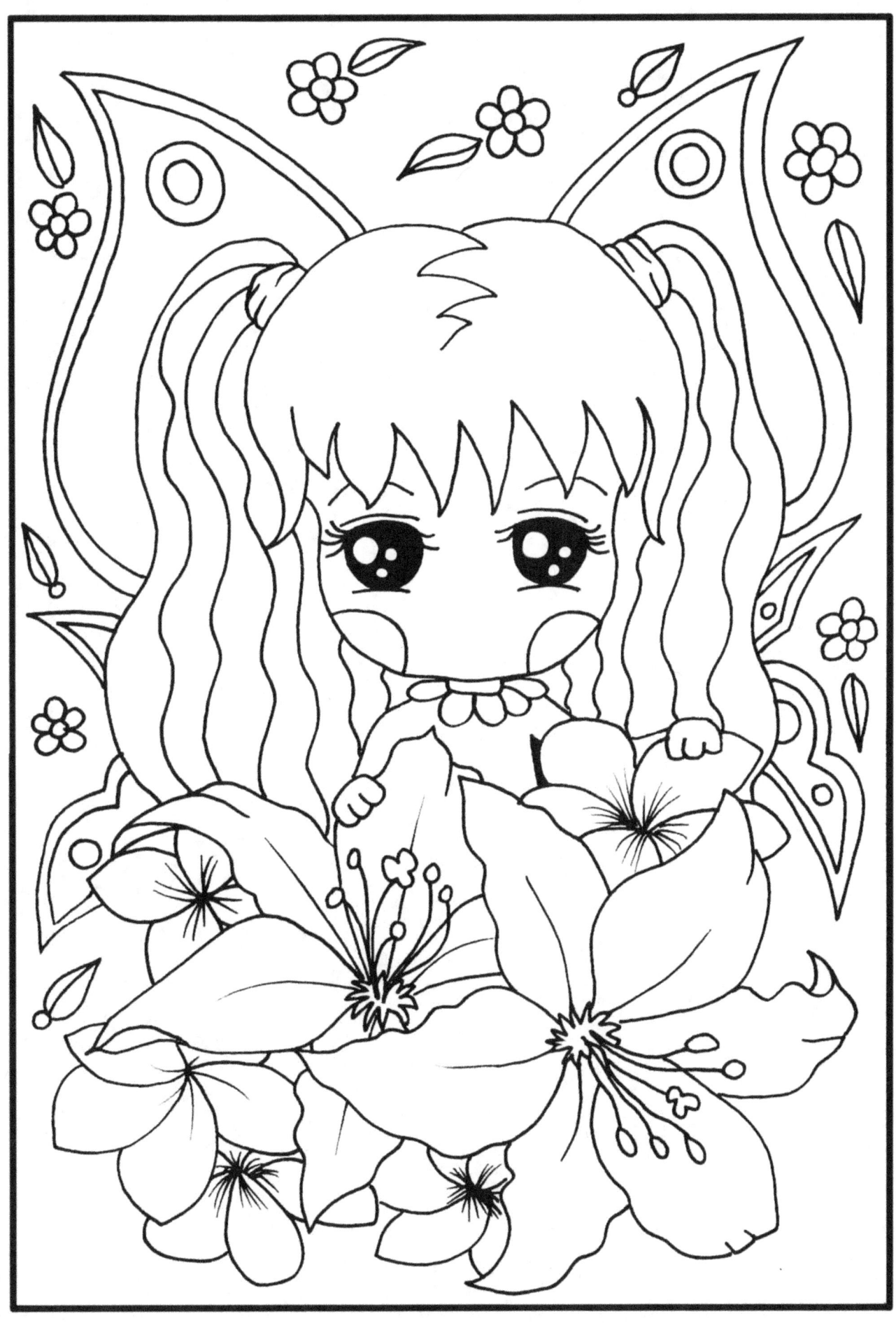

Lottie in the Lillies

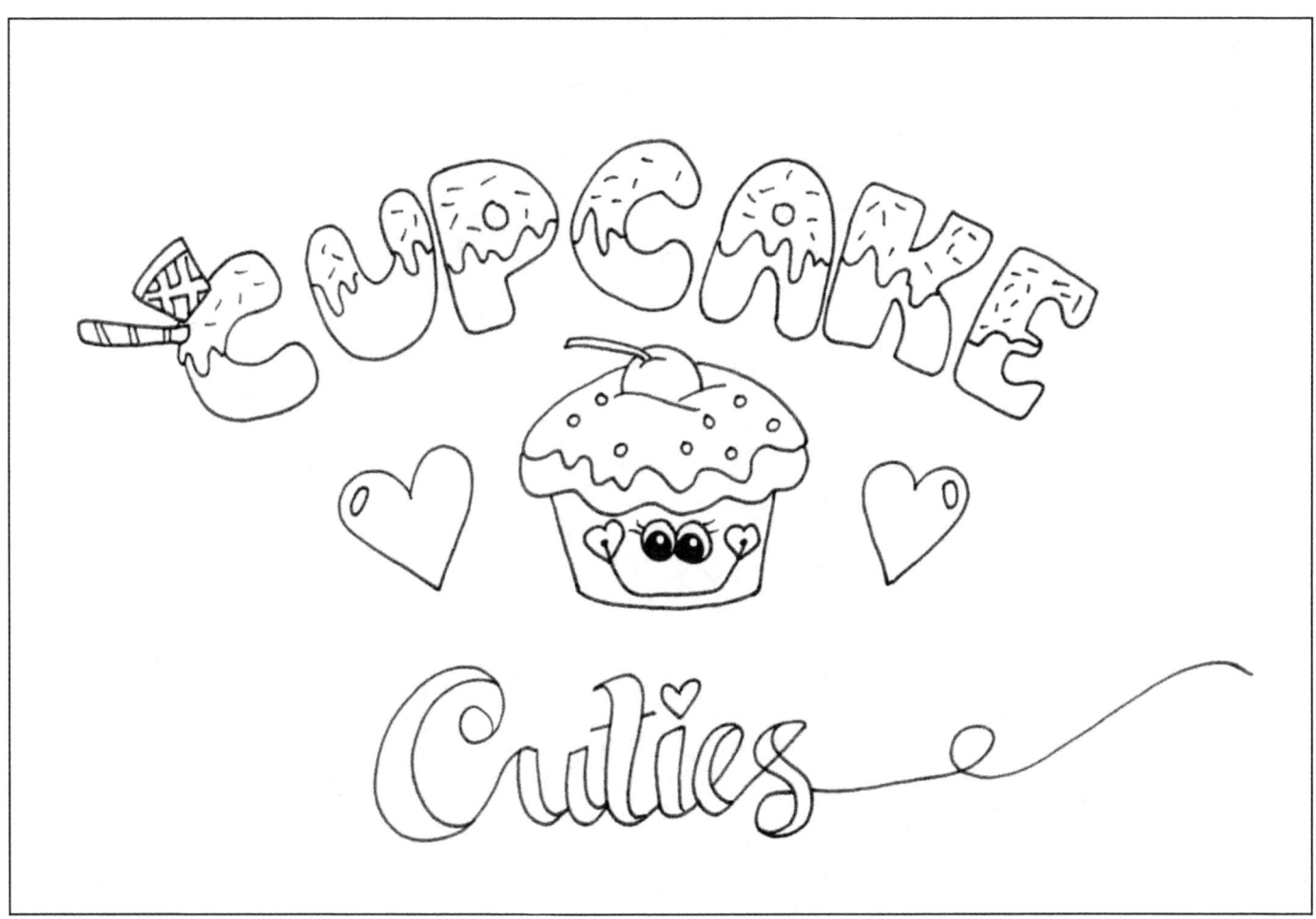

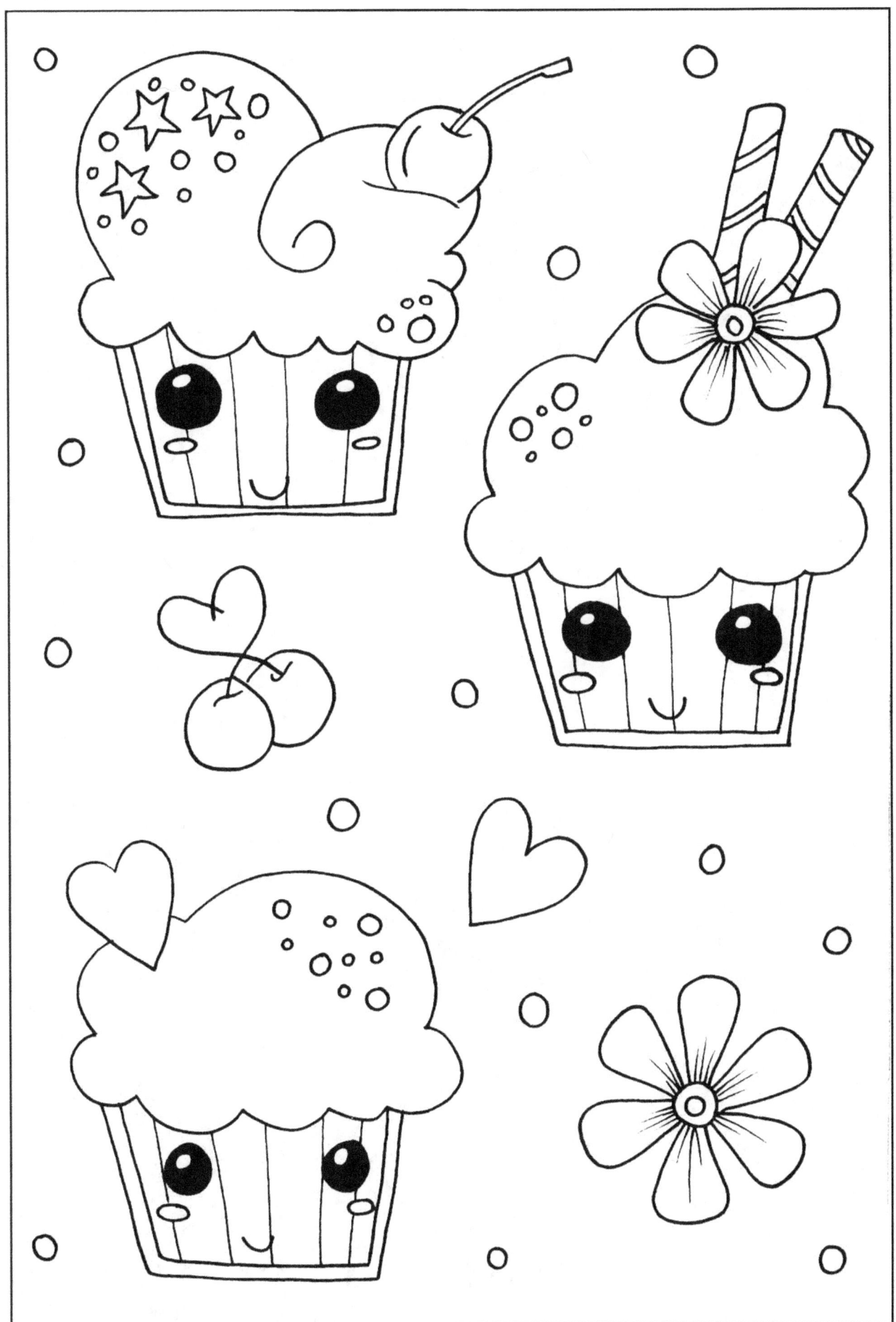

Trio of Treats

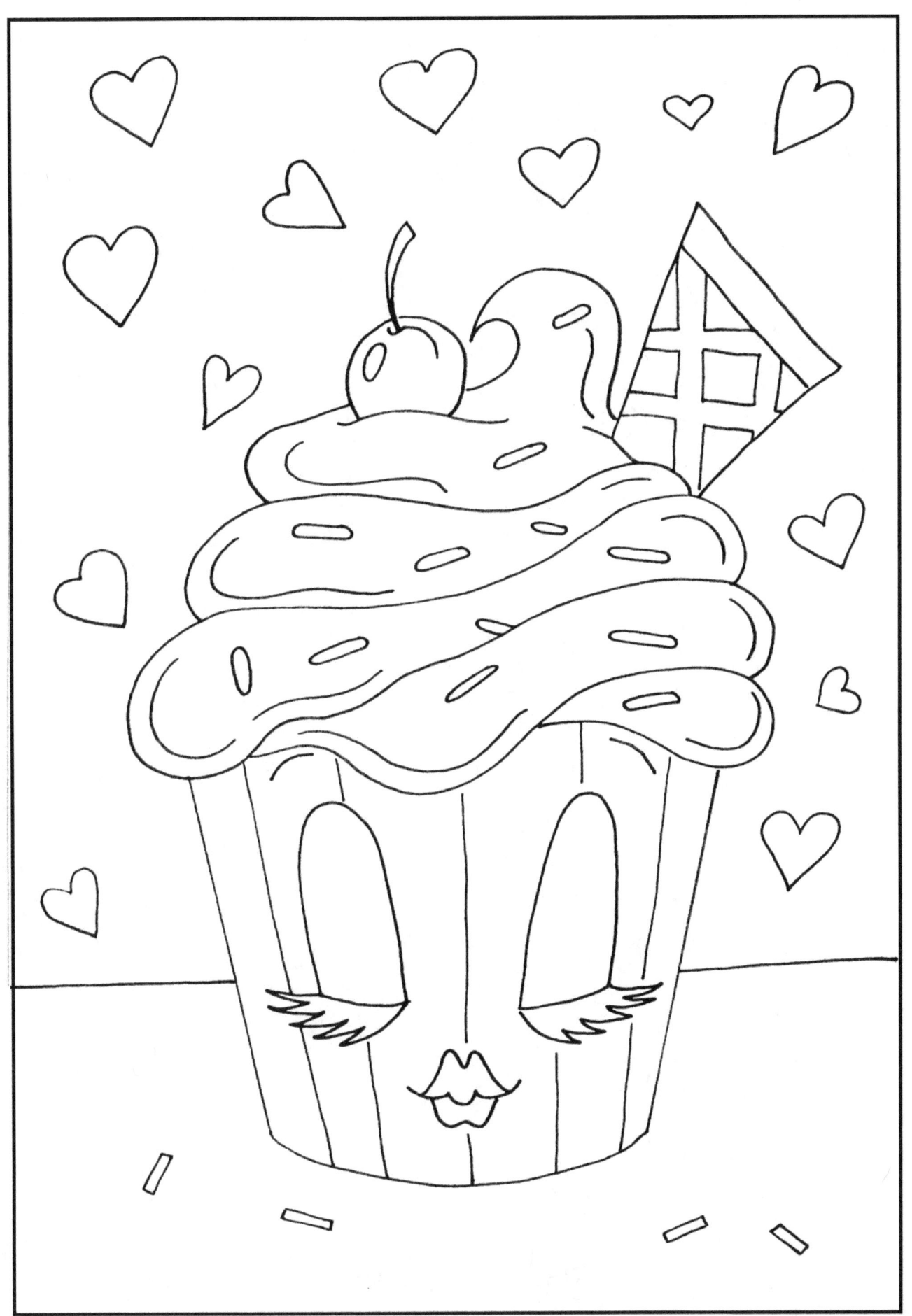

Cassy Cupcake

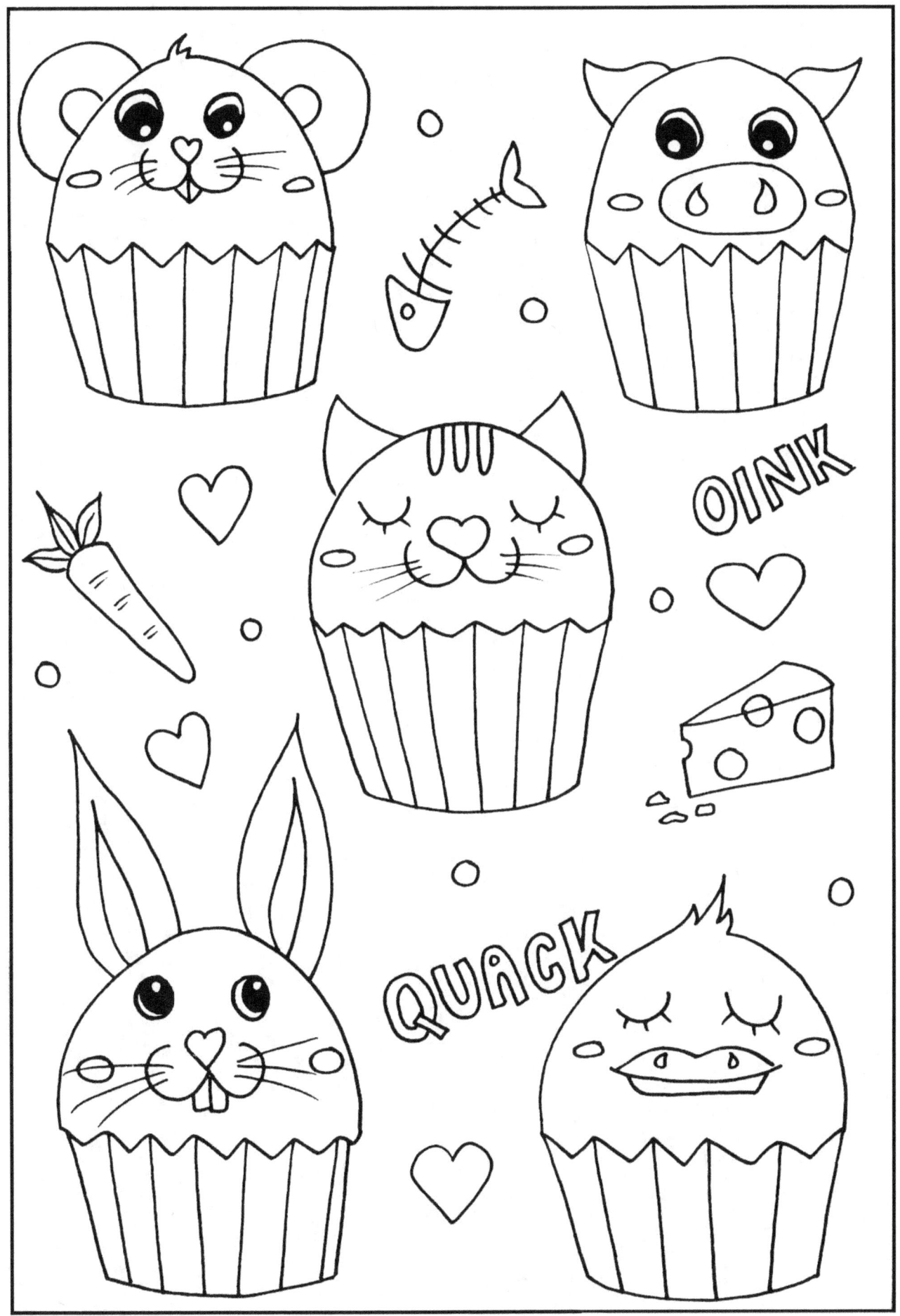

Animal Cupcakes

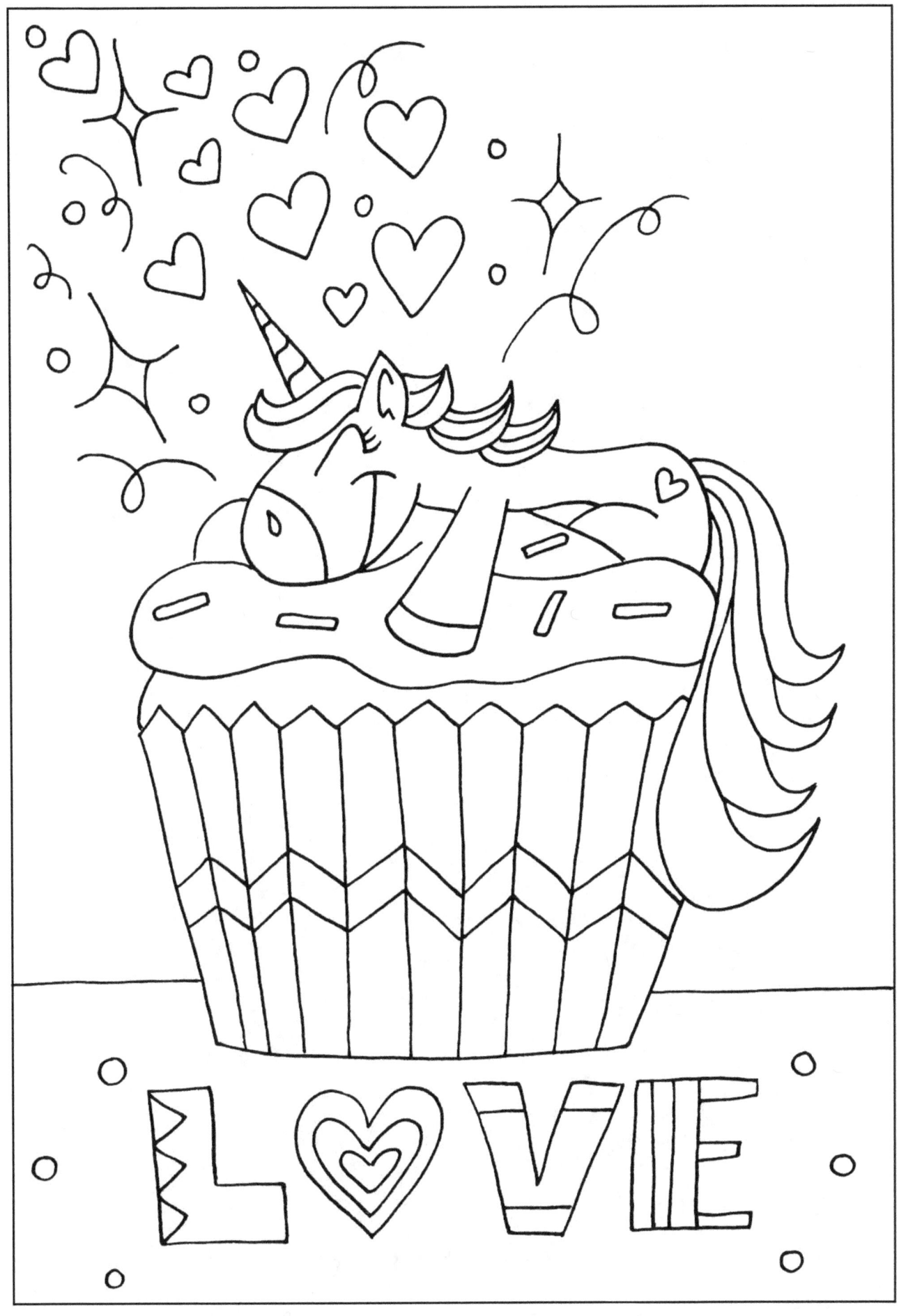

Cupcake Love

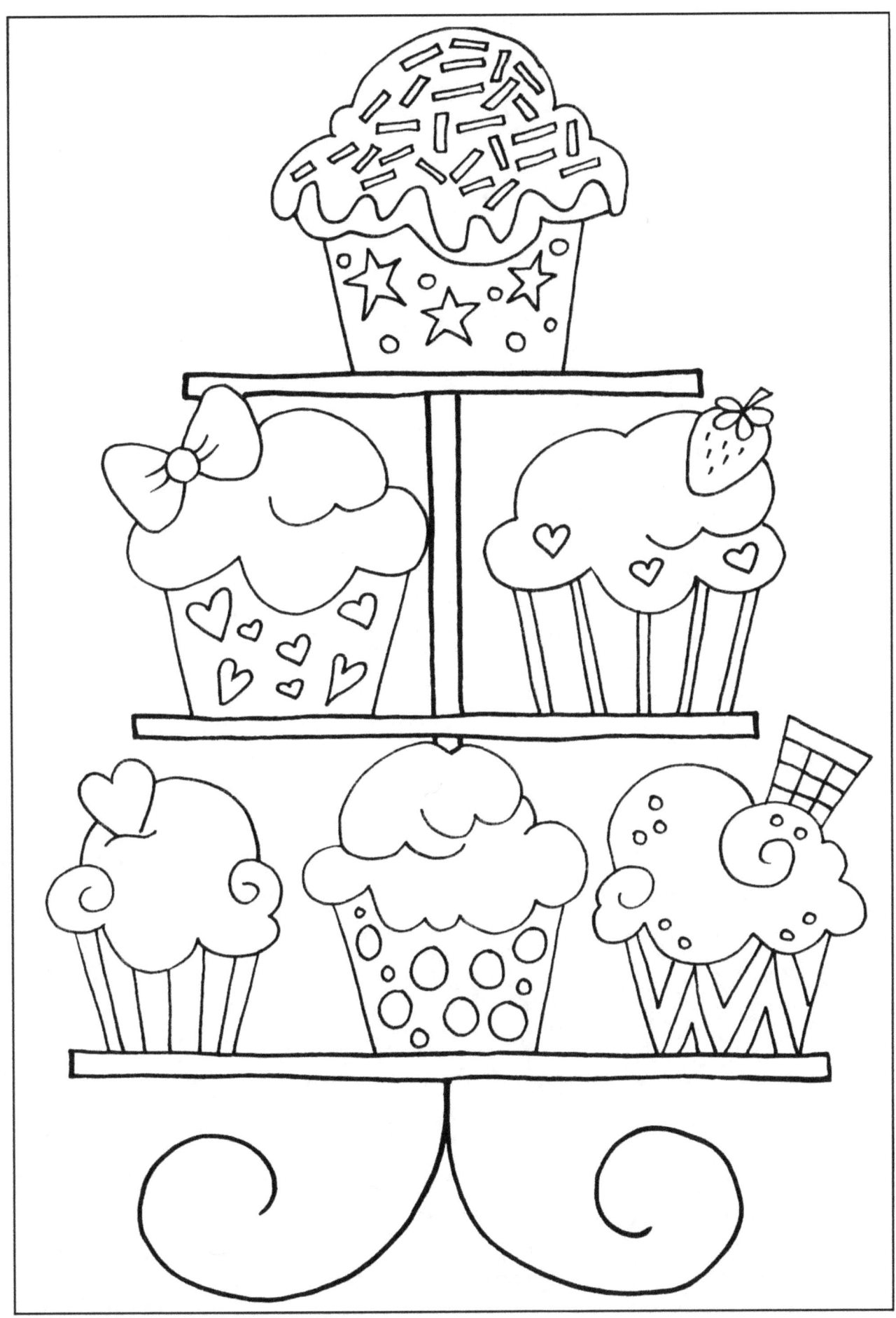

Cupcake Tier

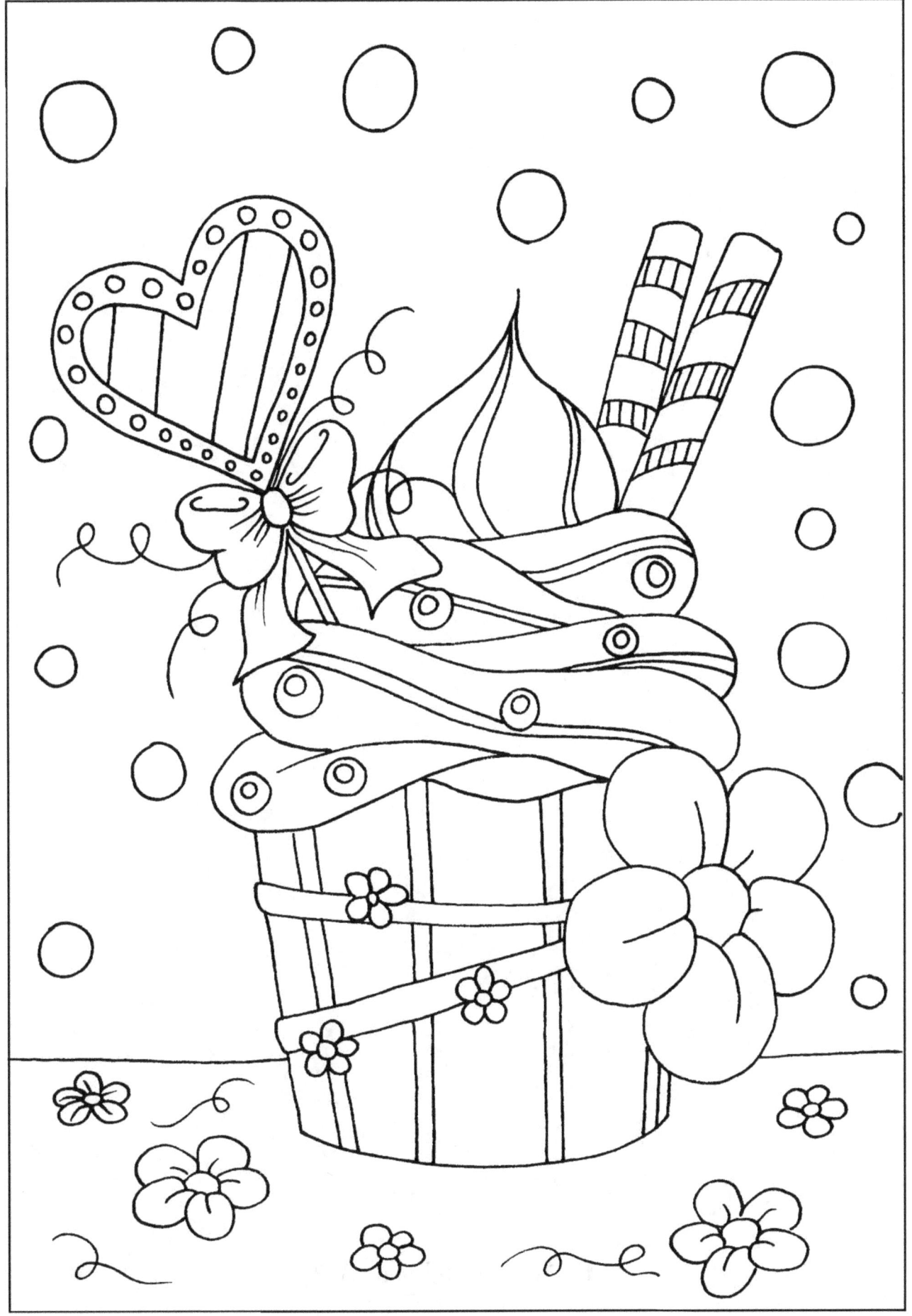

Hearts and Flowers

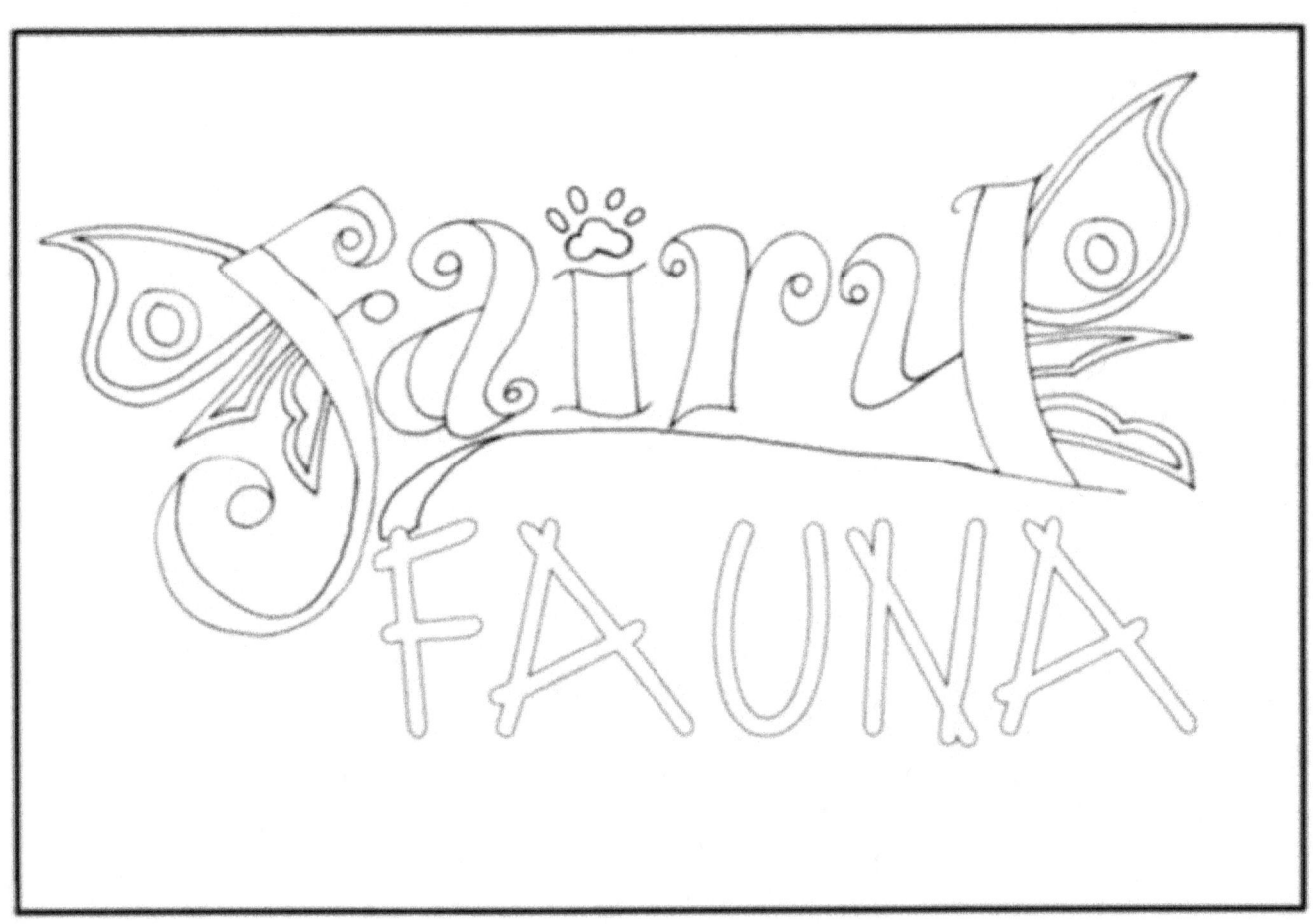

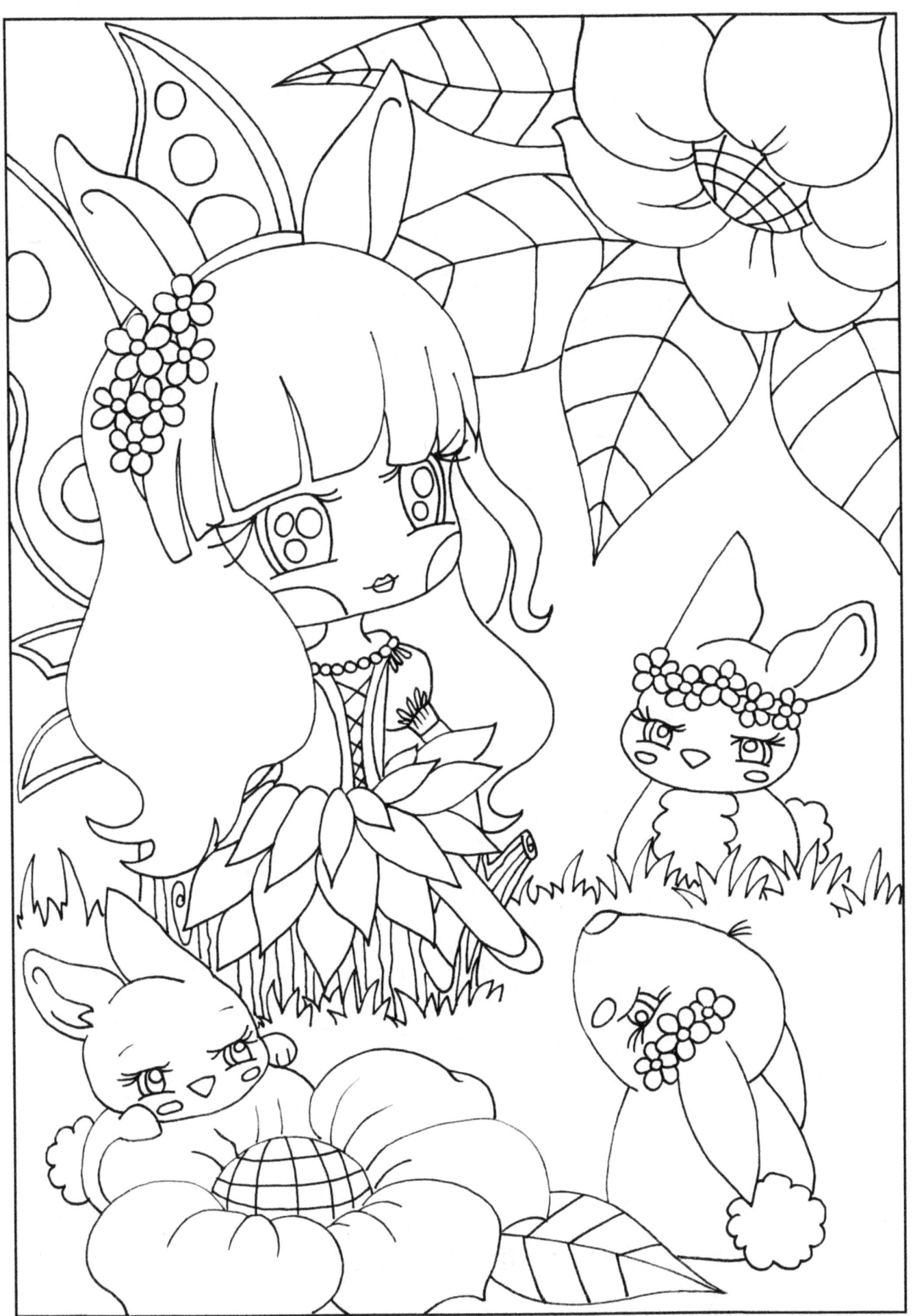

Bonita and her Bunnies

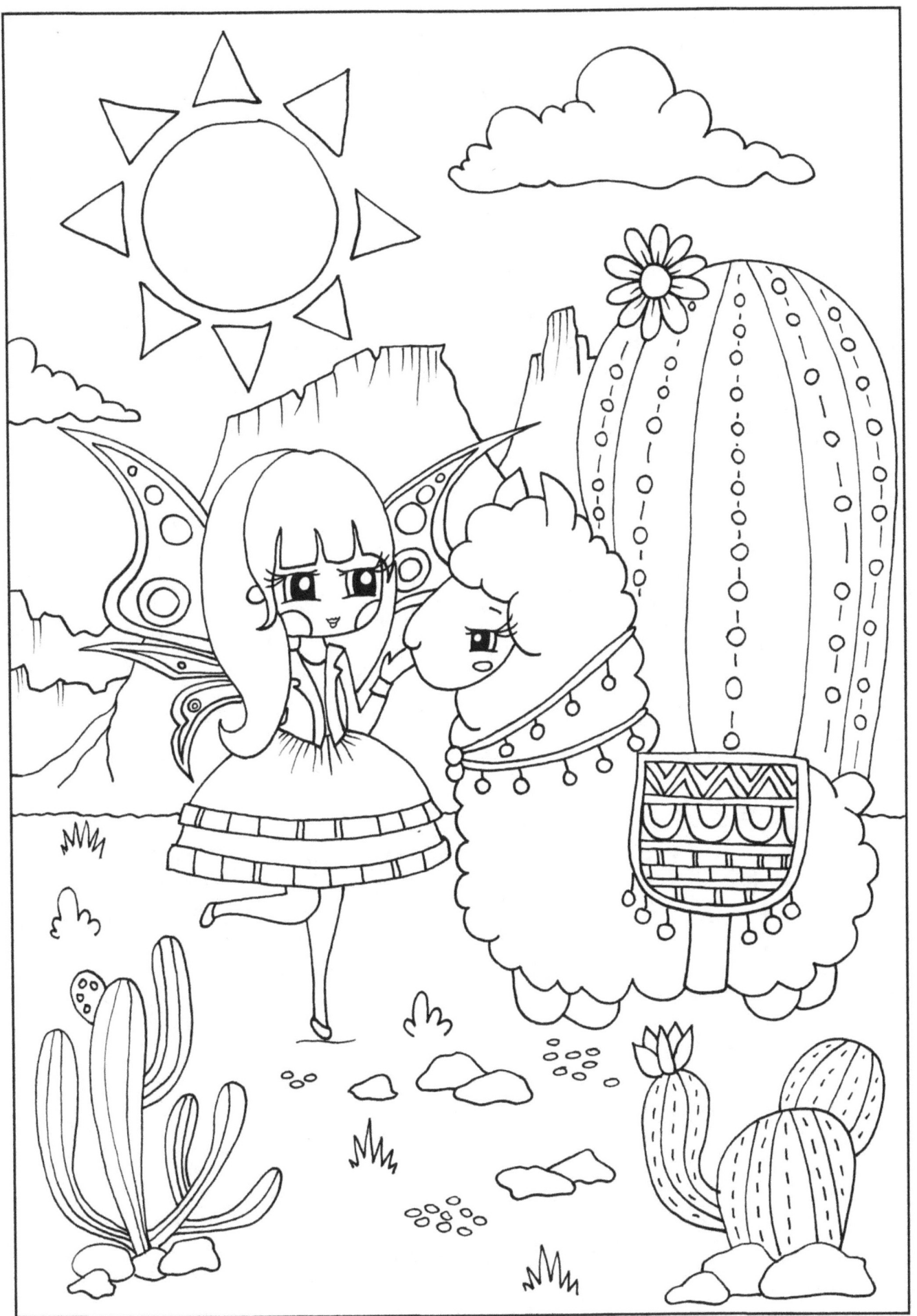

Arizona and her Alpaca

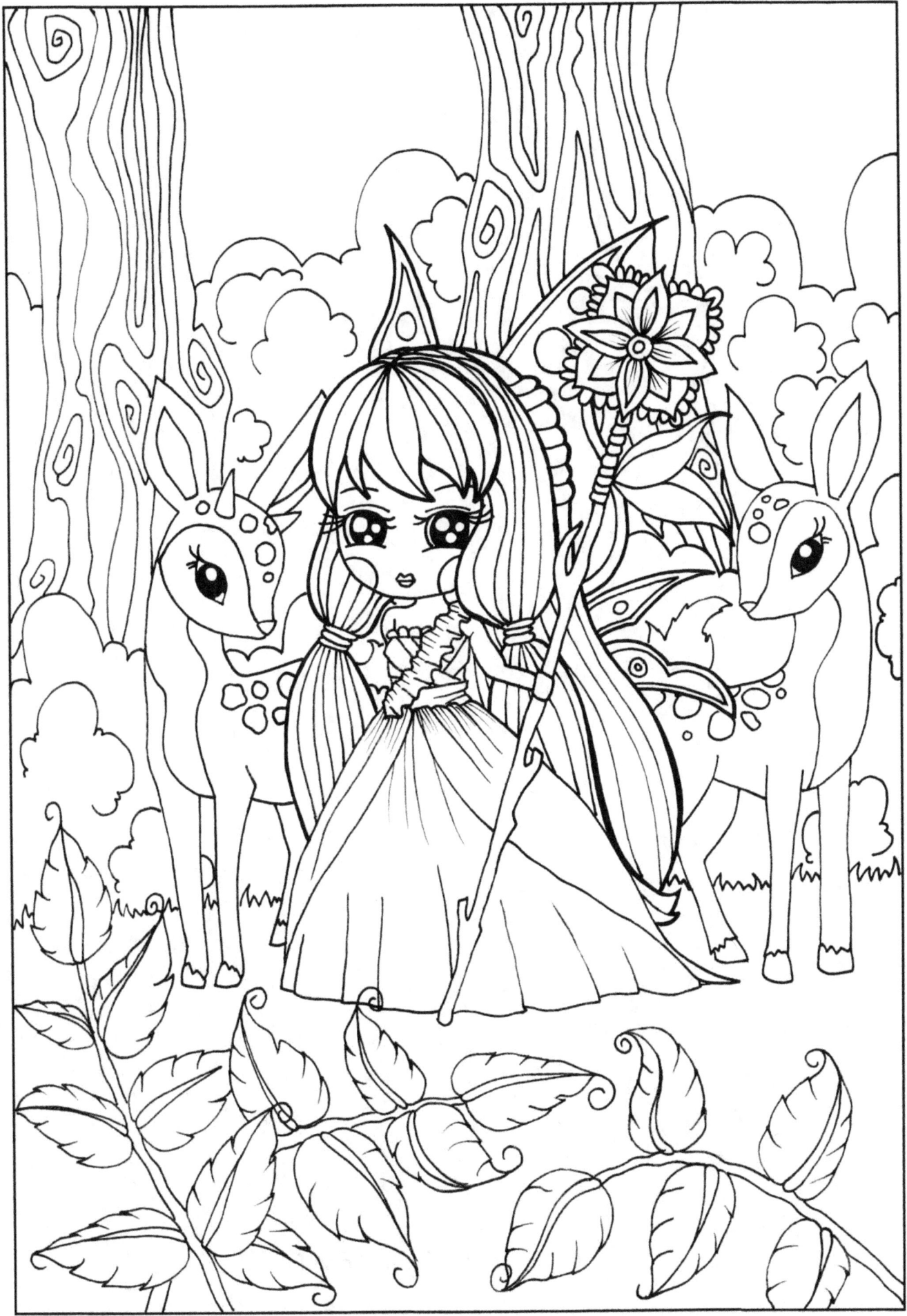

Fawna and her Fawns

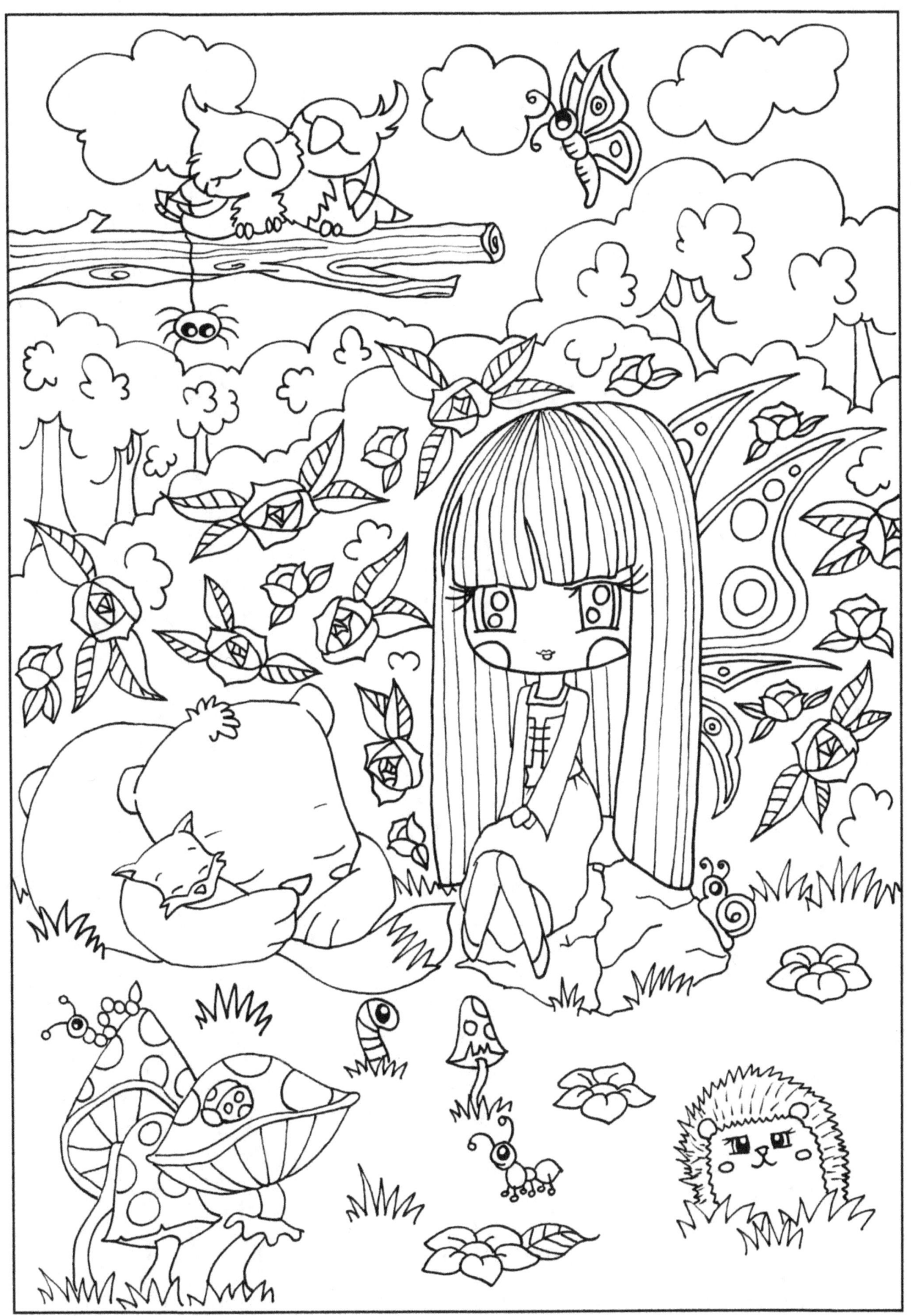

Nina in Nature

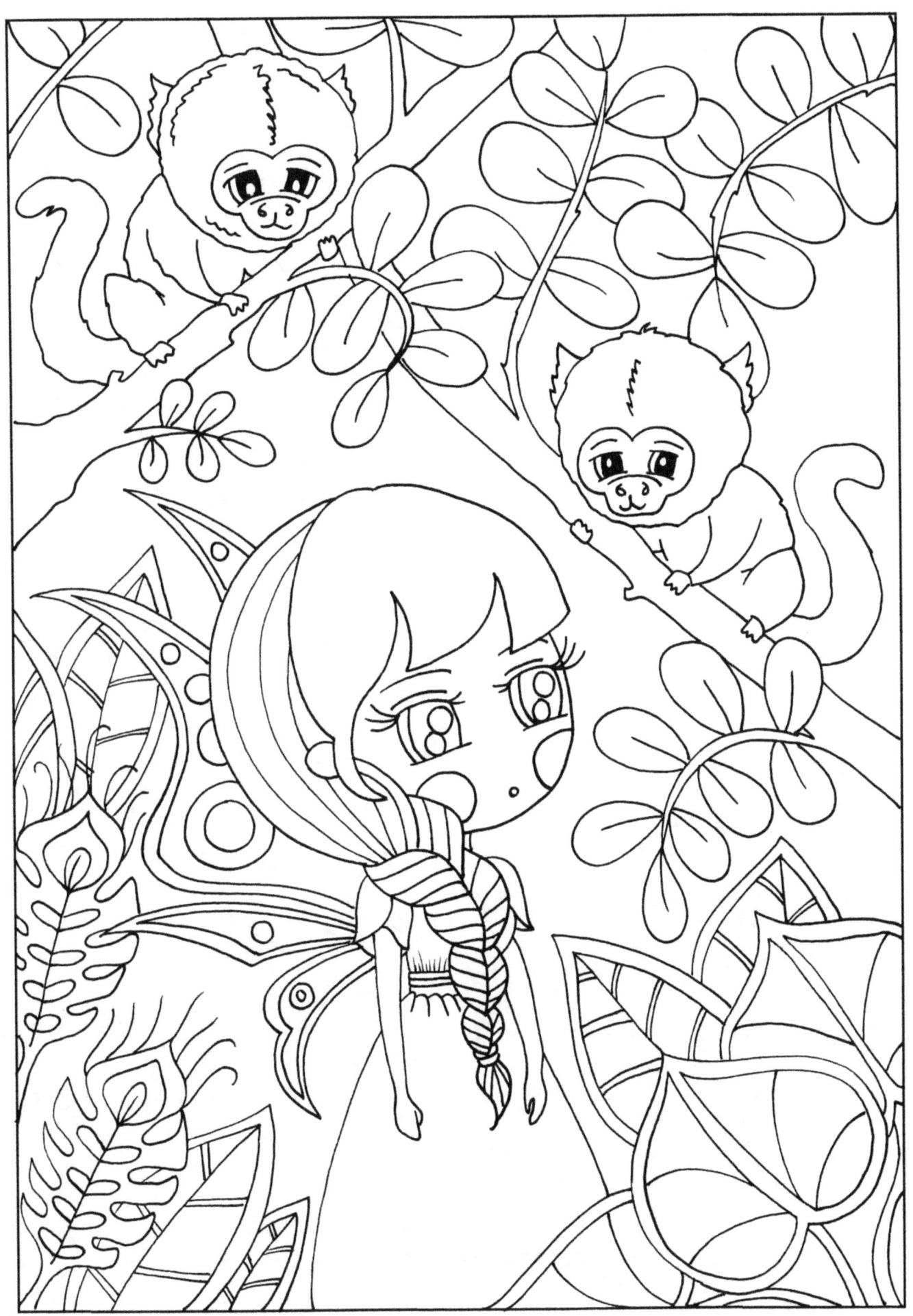

Mera and her monkeys

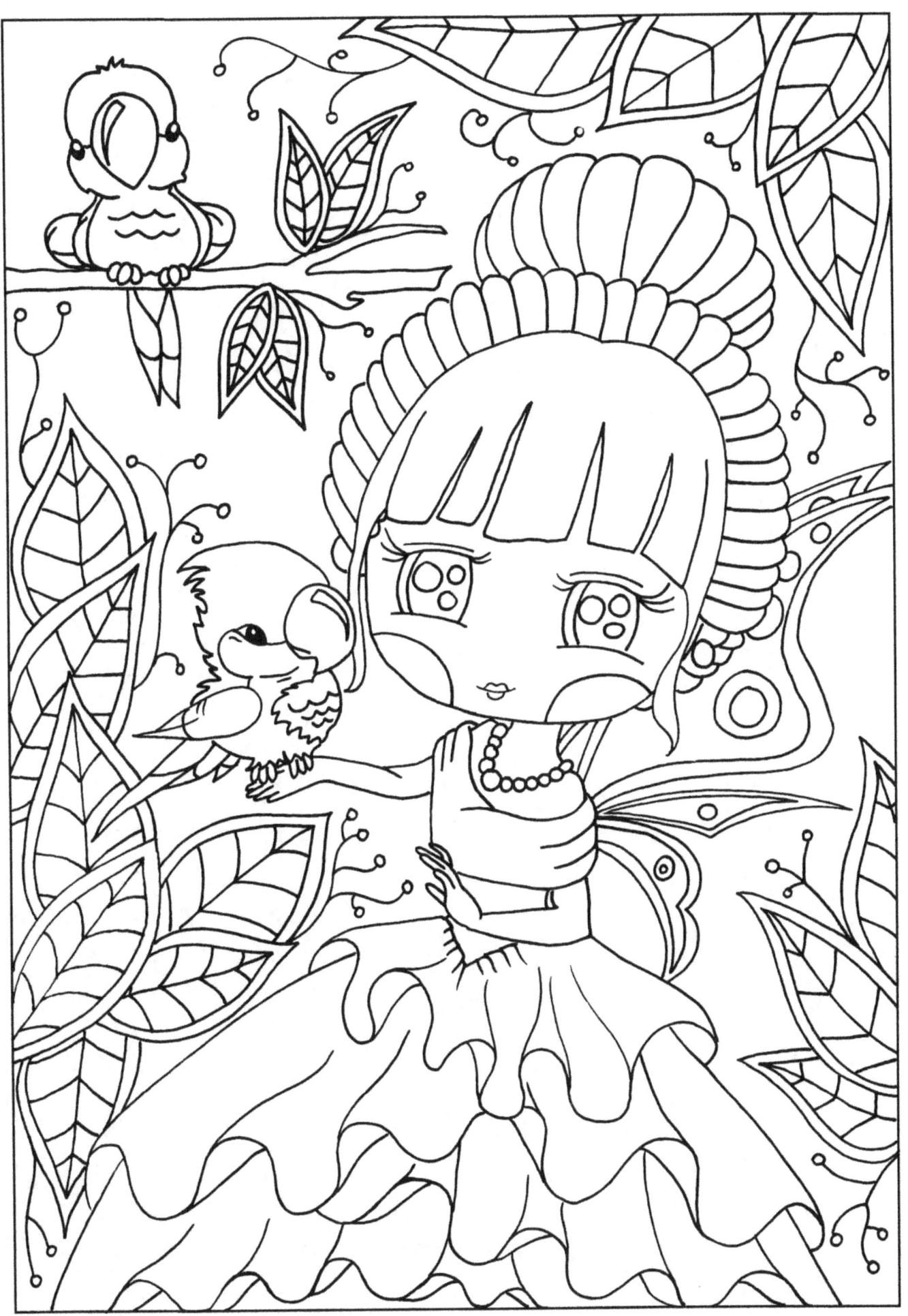

Poppit and her Parrots

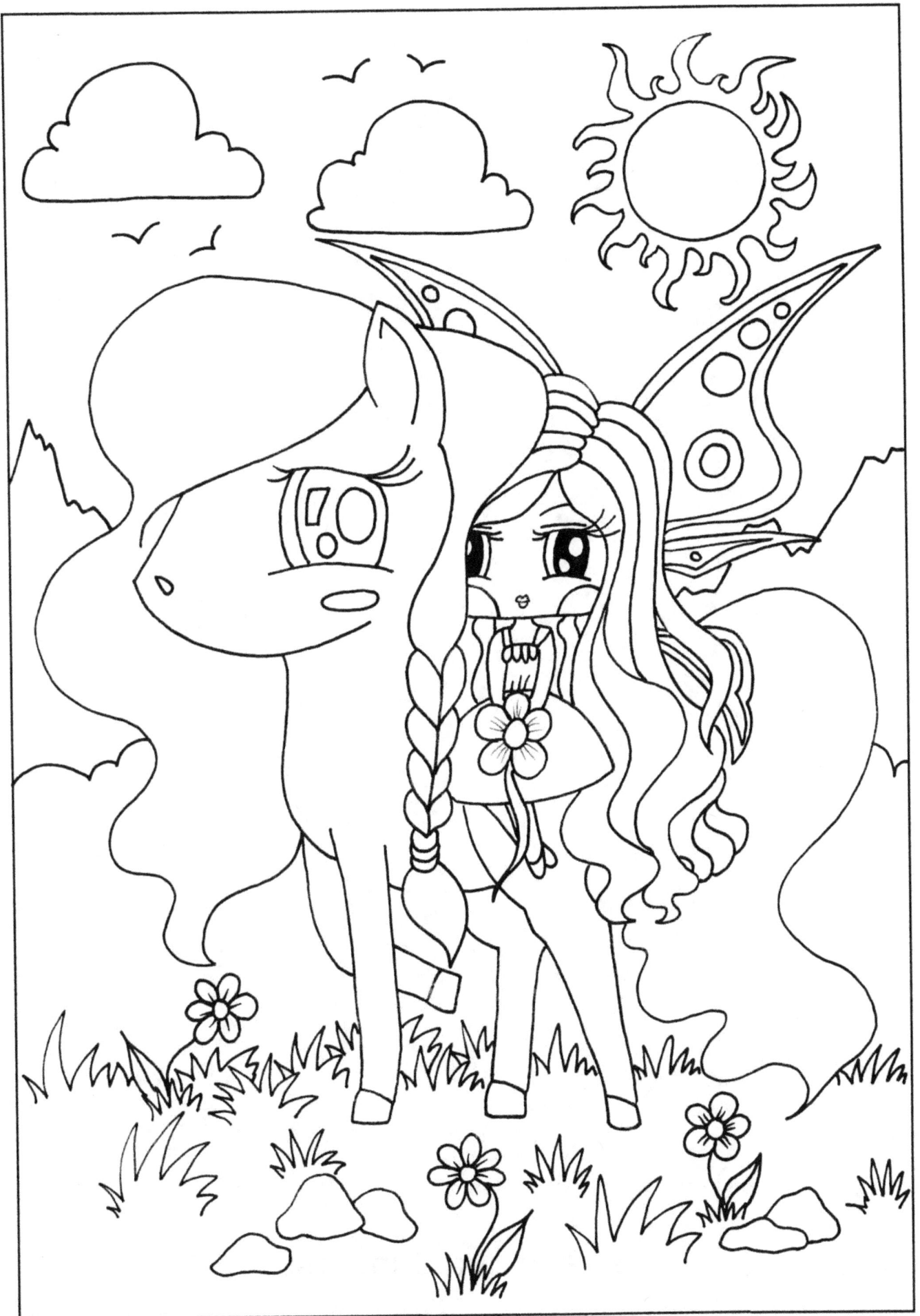

Selene and Sunburst

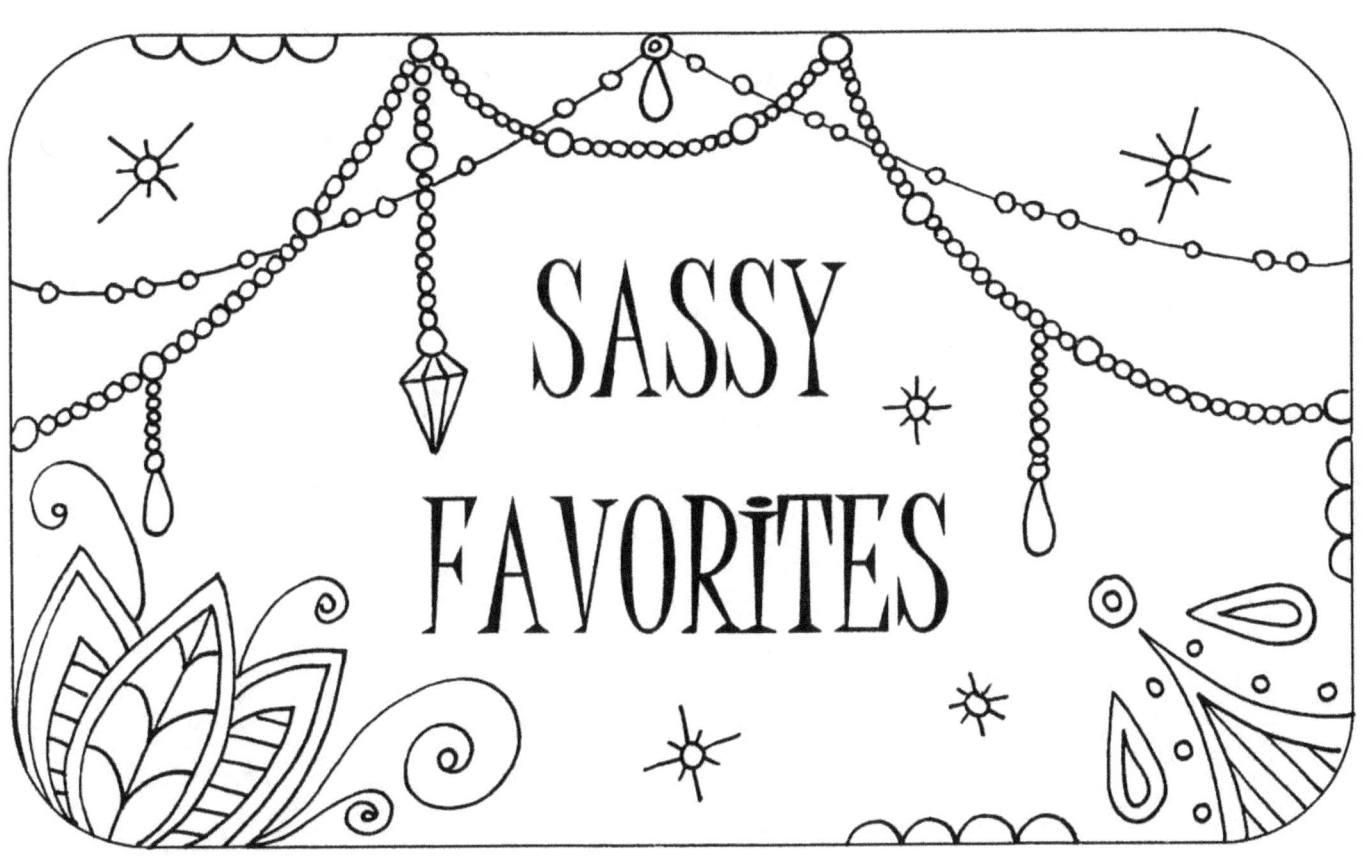

SASSY FAVORITES

Swing in the Stars

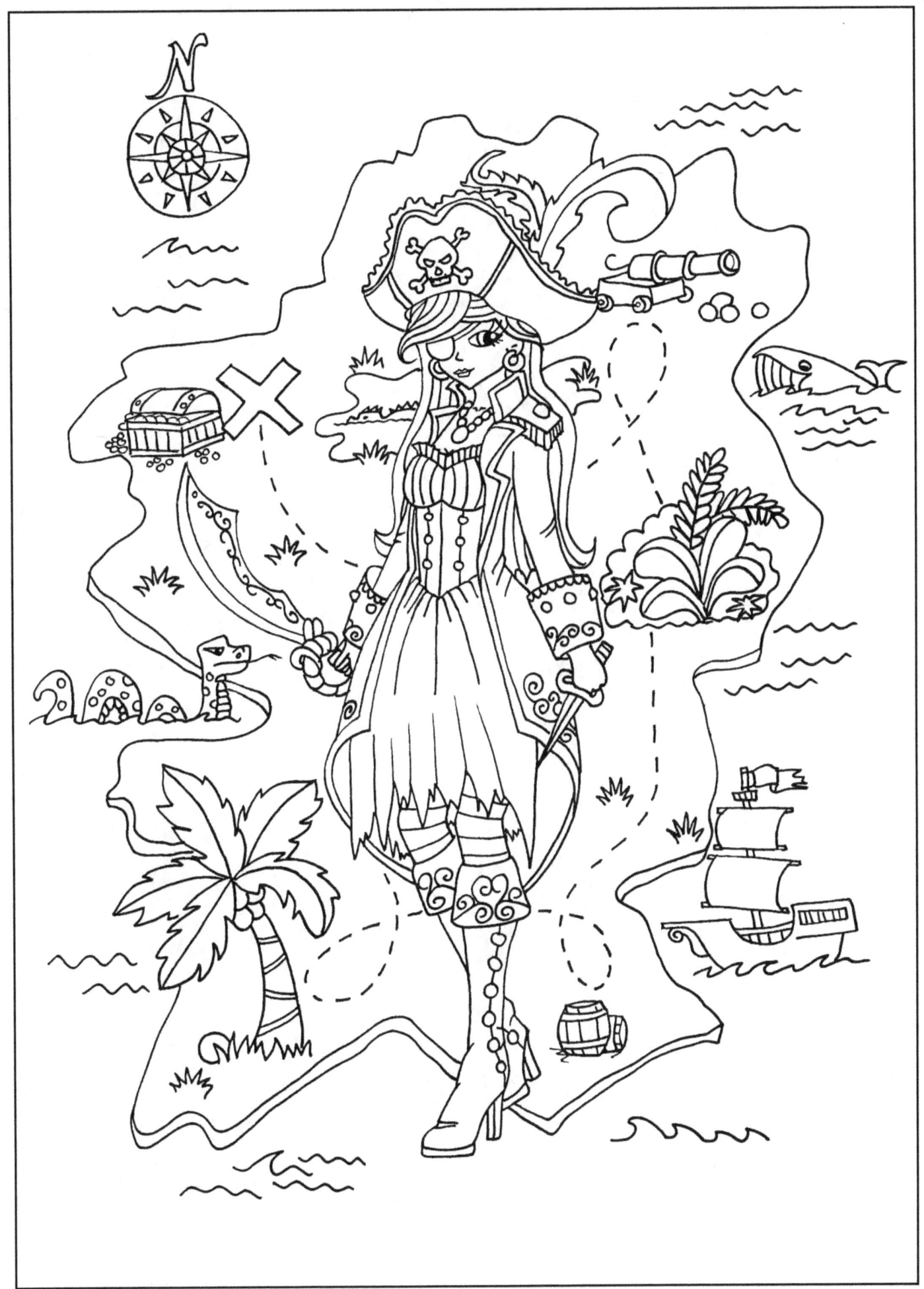

Pirate Ahoy

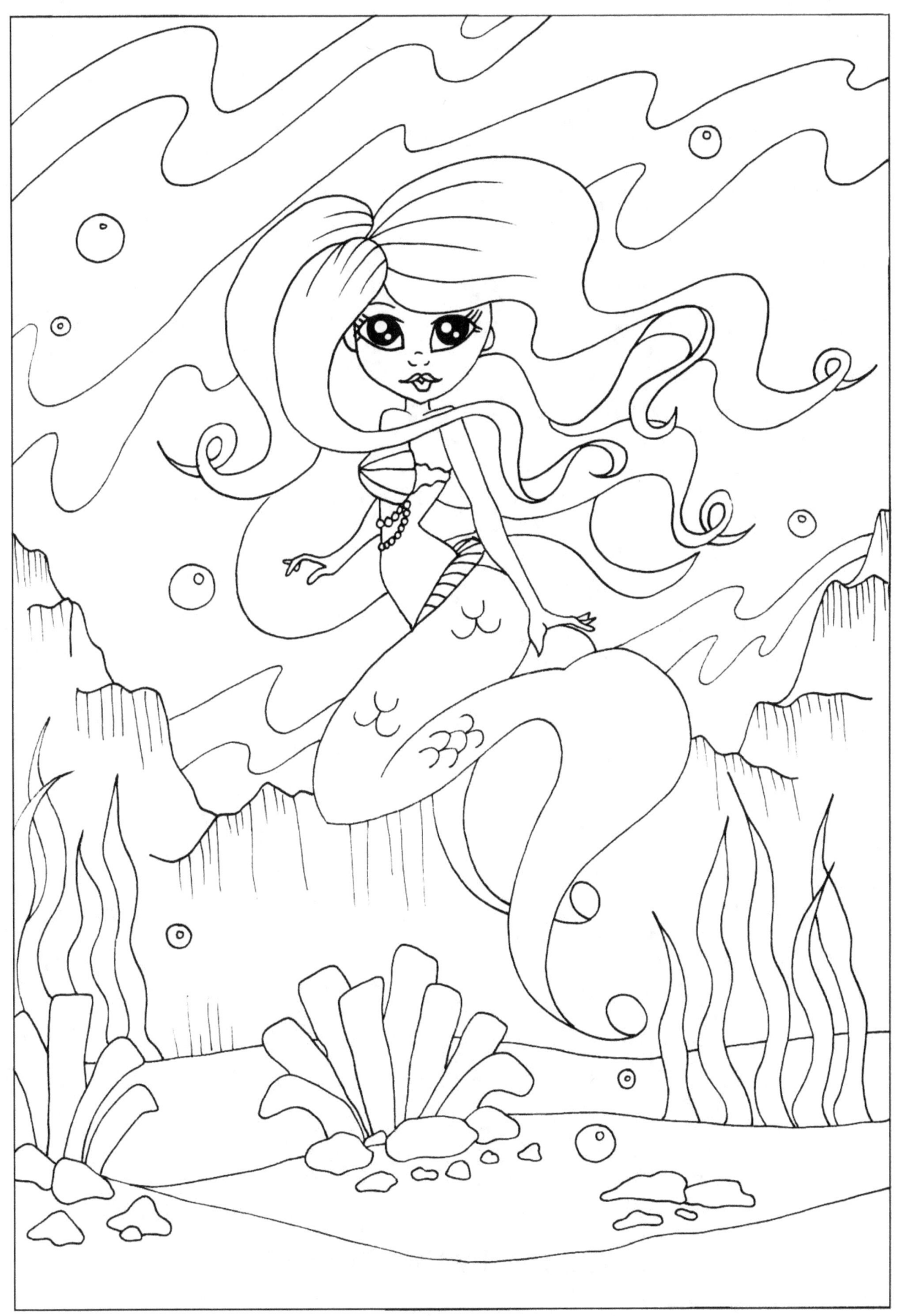

Alone in the Deep

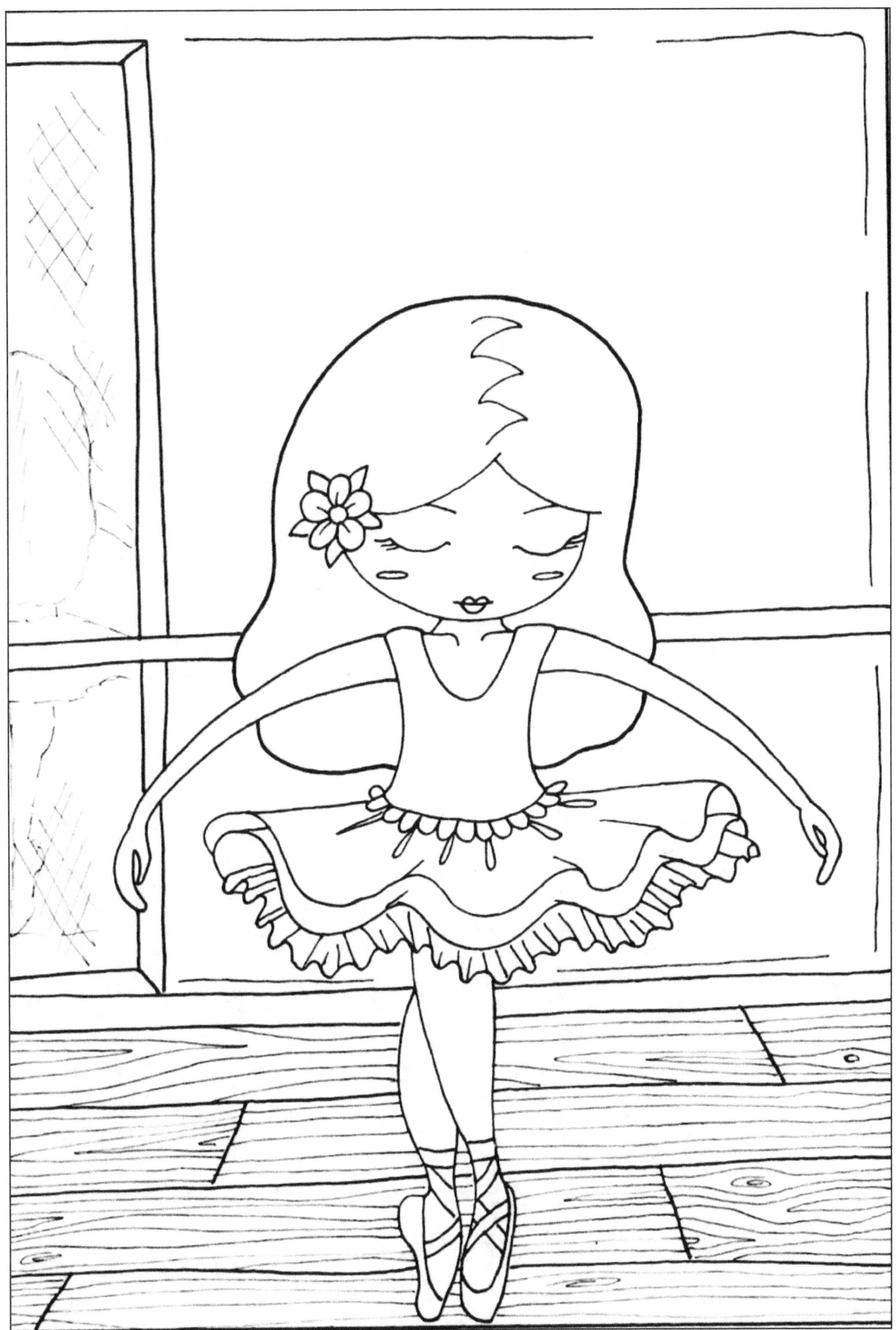

Rehearsals

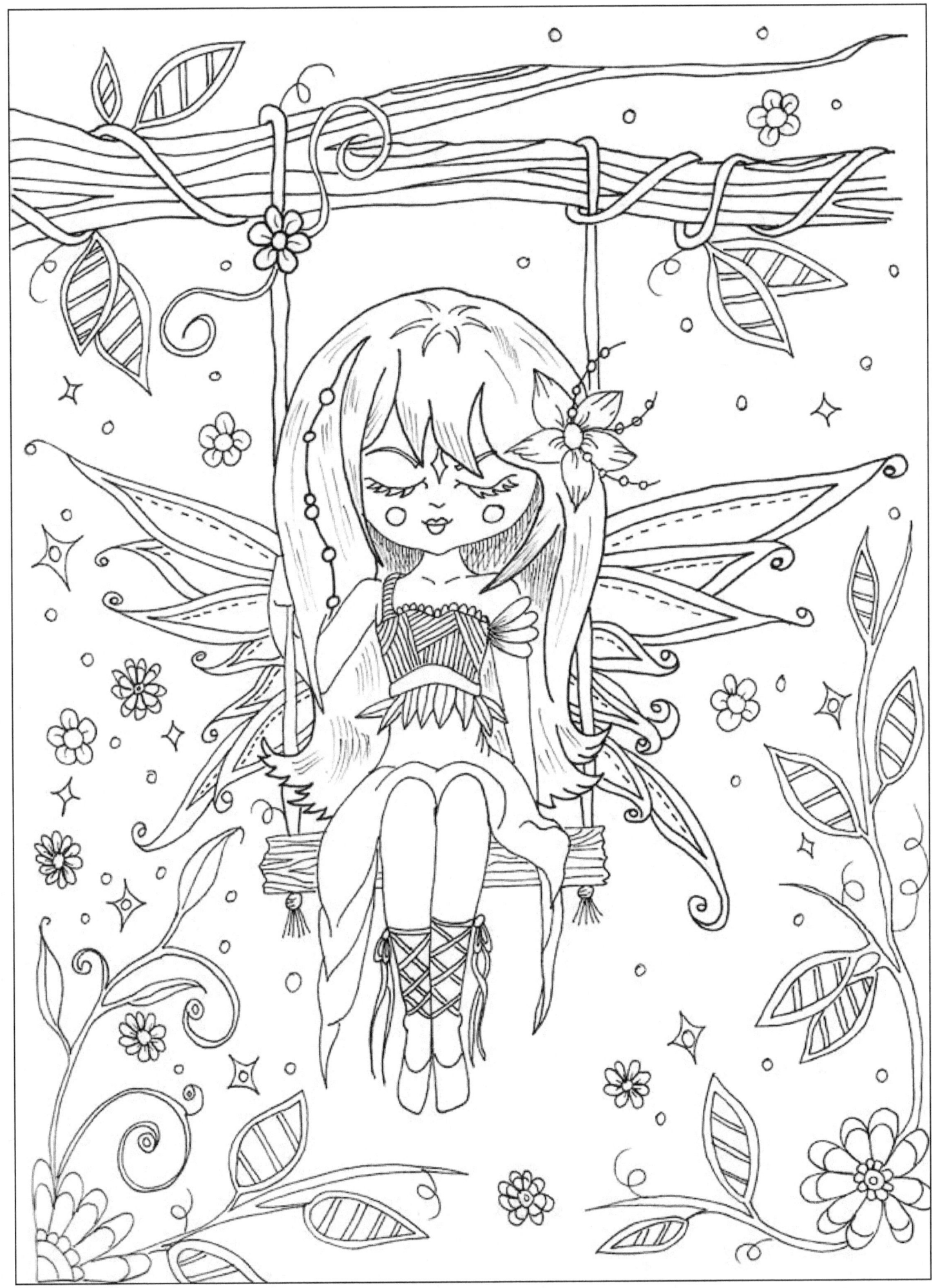

A Fairy Swing

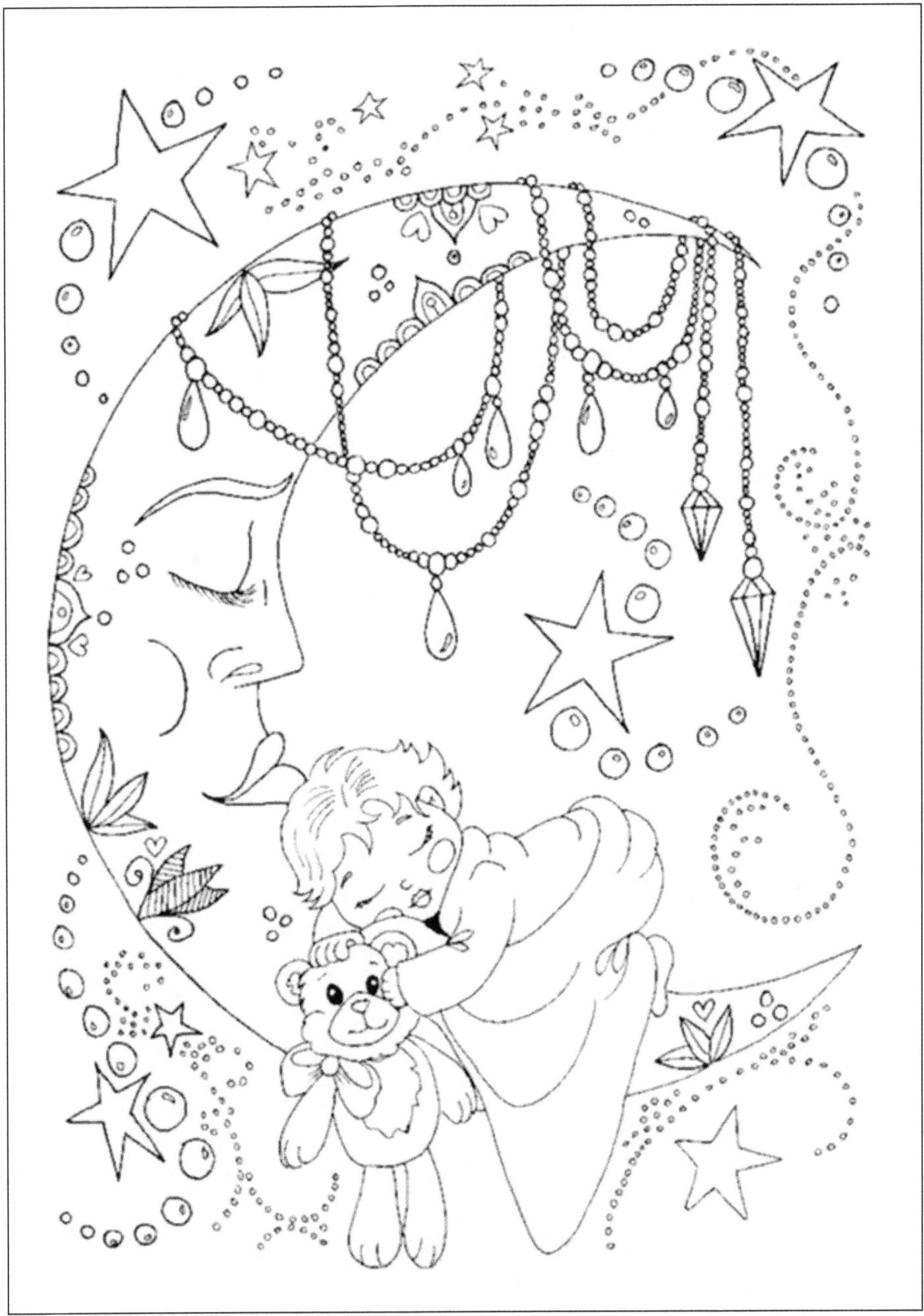

Baby Moon